OSPREY COMBAT AIRCRAFT

MiG-17 AND MiG-19
UNITS OF THE VIETNAM WAR

CW00525975

SERIES EDITOR: TONY HOLMES

OSPREY COMBAT AIRCRAFT • 25

MiG-17 AND MiG-19
UNITS OF THE VIETNAM WAR

Istvân Toperczer

OSPREY
PUBLISHING

Front cover
On 19 July 1966 12 camouflaged, and bombless, F-105D Thunderchiefs of the 355th Tactical Fighter Wing's 354th Tactical Fighter Squadron were detected by ground radar flying over Tam Dao. Armed with missiles only, these machines passed north of Hanoi, bound for Noi Bai airfield. Having headed north unencumbered by bombs, the F-105s were almost certainly on a MiG-hunting mission. They succeeded in their aim of provoking the VPAF's fighter force into action, for at 1450 hrs the 923rd Fighter Regiment's Nguyen Bien and Vo Van Man took off from Noi Bai in their MiG-17s to intercept the incoming USAF fighter-bombers.

The communist pilots quickly engaged four of the F-105s, and Nguyen Bien opened fire. The American pilot targeted by Bien successfully evaded his opening rounds, however, and in turn pulled in behind the MiG. Despite firing numerous bursts of cannon fire at Bien, the 'Thud driver' failed to register any hits.

East of the base Vo Van Man (flying an overall snake-green MiG-17F 'Fresco') latched on to the tail of Bien's pursuer and fired two well-aimed bursts of cannon fire into the F-105. Mortally hit, the Thunderchied (59-1755) crashed before its pilot, 1Lt Steven W Diamond, could eject. The surviving USAF pilots continued to dogfight with the MiGs, but they failed to make any real impression on the agile VPAF fighters. The F-105 pilots were also having to contend with fierce anti-aircraft fire from the flak batteries around Noi Bai.

Two minutes after Diamond had crashed to his death, a second Thunderchief was claimed by Nguyen Bien, while a third F-105 was reportedly hit by flak and exploded over Tuyen Quang. The USAF only officially acknowledge the loss of two F-105s on this sortie, the second having reportedly been downed by AAA. Both MiG-17s recovered safely at Gia Lam airfield in Hanoi (*Cover artwork by Iain Wyllie*)

Previous pages
MiG-17s were still being used alongside MiG-21s at Noi Bai in 1972. No 2072 carries an ORO-57K seven-shot rocket pod, loaded with S-5 (57 mm) unguided rockets, on its port wing pylon (*VNA*)

Dedication
For my son, Ákos

First published in Great Britain in 2001 by Osprey Publishing
Elms Court, Chapel Way, Botley, Oxford, OX2 9LP

© 2001 Osprey Publishing Limited

All rights reserved. Apart from any fair dealing for the purpose of private study, research, criticism or review, as permitted under the Copyright, Design and Patents Act, 1988, no part of this publication may be reproduced, stored in a retrieval system, or transmitted in any form or by any means, electronic, electrical, chemical, mechanical, optical, photocopying, recording or otherwise, without prior written permission. All enquiries should be addressed to the publisher.

ISBN 1 84176 162 1

Edited by Tony Holmes, Neil Maxwell and Peter Mersky
Page design by Mark Holt
Cover Artwork by Iain Wyllie
Aircraft Profiles and Scale Drawings by Mark Styling
Origination by Grasmere Digital Imaging, Leeds, UK
Printed in Hong Kong through Bookbuilders

00 01 02 03 04   10 9 8 7 6 5 4 3 2 1

EDITOR'S NOTE
To make this best-selling series as authoritative as possible, the Editor would be interested in hearing from any individual who may have relevant photographs, documentation or first-hand experiences relating to the world's combat aircraft, and the crews that flew them, in the various theatres of war. Any material used will be credited to its original source. Please write to Tony Holmes at 10 Prospect Road, Sevenoaks, Kent, TN13 3UA, Great Britain, or by e-mail at: tony.holmes@osprey-jets.freeserve.co.uk

ACKNOWLEDGEMENTS
The Author would like to thank the following individuals and organisations for their help and support with this project – W Howard Plunkett, Tony Morris, Nguyen Van Coc, Nguyen Van Dinh, Dao Hoang Giang, Trung H Huynh, Tran Dinh Kiem, Truong Van Minh, Nguyen Viet Phuc, Pham Tuan, József Beke, Ernö Bohár, Sándor Doma, Tibor Hajdü, István Karancz, Sándor Legoza, Gábor Pálfai, Imre Pet›, Zoltán Pintér, Gábor Szekeres, József Vanyó, the museums of the Vietnamese People's Air Force, the Embassy of the Socialist Republic of Vietnam in Budapest, the Embassy of Hungary in Hanoi, and the Ministry of Foreign Affairs of the Socialist Republic of Vietnam in Hanoi.

For a catalogue of all Osprey Publishing titles please contact us at:

Osprey Direct UK, PO Box 140, Wellingborough, Northants NN8 4ZA, UK
E-mail: **info@ospreydirect.co.uk**

Osprey Direct USA, c/o Motorbooks International, 729 Prospect Ave, PO Box 1, Osceola, WI 54020, USA
E-mail: **info@ospreydirectusa.com**

Or visit our website: **www.ospreypublishing.com**

CONTENTS

INTRODUCTION

The Vietnamese People's Air Force – Khong Quan Nhan Dan Viet Nam – began life in the 1940s virtually from scratch, its development being helped by supportive communist countries such as the USSR and China. Yet despite the aid of these superpowers, when hostilities with America really heated up in 1964, the VPAF had only one regiment of MiG-17 fighters with which to 'welcome' the USAF and US Navy aircraft (superior in numbers and technology) that were pushing into their airspace. By the end of the war, however, things were different, and the VPAF had at hand a considerable number of aircraft of much better quality.

Although the Americans always enjoyed a numerical advantage throughout the conflict, resulting in the North Vietnamese suffering considerable losses, US pilots always had to be on the look-out for a MiG appearing out of nowhere and pressing home an attack. In the long years that the adversaries fought it out in the air, both sides changed their tactics several times. Some strategies worked, others didn't. But one thing the air war achieved perhaps above all else was a fundamental change in the principles of the use of air power, as well as ensuring a considerable boost to aircraft design, technical development and manufacture.

For the VPAF, the journey it had to undertake from the first propeller-driven flight to the first time one of its airmen broke through the sound barrier was a long one, and a tough one. However, the experiences the air force gained along the way provide important lessons even today for every young pilot longing to strap himself into a MiG.

VIETNAMESE ICARUS

When the former Emperor Bao Dai arrived in Hanoi as an advisor to the Democratic Republic of Vietnam after the revolt against the French colonial regime in August 1945, he was the proud owner of two light aircraft.

Dai had been the last Emperor of the Nguyen Dynasty, reigning from 1926 to 1945, when he abdicated in favour of Ho Chi Minh and fled to France. In 1949 he returned from self-imposed exile in Hong Kong to resume his status as emperor under French and American sponsorship. Bao Dai proved less than successful in this new role, however, being corrupt, and still lacking fluency in Vietnamese due to his classical French education.

Despite these failings, he represented acceptable Vietnamese 'nationalism' in the eyes of the French and American governments, who vehemently opposed Ho Chi Minh and his Viet Minh communist revolutionaries. Bao Dai remained in power for another four years, before being deposed by the newly-elected Prime Minister of South Vietnam, Ngo Dinh Diem, in 1954 and fleeing to France. He died in Paris in July 1997.

Returning to the emperor's aircraft, Bao Dai owned a British-built Tiger Moth two-seat biplane trainer and a French Morane-Saulnier

parasol monoplane. Both had been owned by French pilots who fled when the revolt began in 1945, leaving the aircraft idle in storage. Bao Dai, who had a taste for a racy and sporty lifestyle, inherited them.

At the end of that year Bao Dai offered the aircraft to the revolutionaries, suggesting they be taken to Hanoi from Hué. The government was keen to accept his offer, and liked the suggestion that they could be used to teach young people to fly. Bao Dai also hoped to have the chance to use them privately. The Ministry of Defence entrusted Phan Phac, head of the Department of Military Training, and a pre-revolutionary French Army veteran, to bring the aircraft north.

Dismantled and shipped to Hanoi by train, the aircraft duly completed their journey by road to an airfield in the Tung Thien district of Son Tay (now Ha Tay province). There, they could be kept out of harm's way, clear of the larger airfields including Gia Lam, Bach Mai and Cat Bi that had been occupied by the Chinese army, which had entered North Vietnam to disarm the Japanese at the end of World War 2.

In January 1946 the Tiger Moth and Morane-Saulnier reached Tong airfield, accompanied by a maintenance crew headed by mechanic Tran Dong. But the crew encountered problems and the aircraft remained in their packing cases. In December, when the revolt against the French erupted into a full-scale war of national resistance, the little aircraft might

Permanently grounded through the removal of its outer wing sections, Emperor Bao Dai's Morane-Saulnier parasol monoplane was used as a trainer for Vietnamese pilots and mechanics from March 1949 onwards (*VPAF Museum*)

have played a part against their former owners. Indeed, it was suggested that the Morane-Saulnier should be used to drop mortars on French forces in Nam Dinh. However, the idea was rejected, and the Joint General Staff were ordered by the revolutionary leaders to take the aircraft to the base at Viet Bac. After a long journey by land and water, they ended up in Chiem Hoa, where a corn field was used as a temporary airstrip.

The aircraft might also have eventually found themselves back in their packing cases had it not been for a decree from Ho Chi Minh himself, Vietnam's revolutionary leader. On his orders, the Ministry of Defence formed the Air Force Research Committee (Ban Nghien Cuu Khong Quan) on 9 March 1949. The Tiger Moth and Morane-Saulnier became valuable trainers for pilots and mechanics.

Nguyen Duc Viet was among the first officers assigned to the committee. He was a soldier of German nationality (his mother was German and his father Vietnamese, and he grew up in Germany) who had served in the French *Légion Étrangère*, the famed and feared Foreign Legion. Viet had switched his allegiance to the revolutionary fighters in the early days of the conflict in Trung Bo (central Vietnam).

On the afternoon of 15 August 1949, Viet prepared for a flight in the Tiger Moth, and took off smoothly from Son Dung sand bar beside the Gam River, with mechanic Tran Dong as his passenger. The aircraft reached an altitude of more than 3000 ft, but developed mechanical problems during the descent. Only Viet's skill saved their lives.

The aircraft was a write-off, but that mattered little, for the flight was to go down in history as the first time a Vietnamese aircraft, bearing the Vietnamese insignia, had flown in the free air space of the Democratic Republic of Vietnam.

THE NIGHTFIGHTER

In September 1963 Lt Chert Saibory, a Thai national serving with the Royal Laotian Air Force, was taking part in an air display. But the routine he had in mind was different to anything that anyone watching from the ground might have expected. He defected, flying his T-28 Trojan to North Vietnam and offering his services to the communist government in Hanoi.

Saibory was immediately placed in prison upon his arrival in North Vietnam, and his aircraft stored at the A-33 Aircraft Repair Facility (the VPAF's primary maintenance base) for six months. It was then refurbished and commissioned as the air force's first fighter aircraft.

In 1963 and 1964, the Americans flew reconnaissance flights over North Vietnam by day and by night, dropping propaganda leaflets and sending in special forces. The pattern of US operations was closely studied by senior air force personnel under Col-Gen Dang Tinh, and a plan was prepared to counter them. At last a special use had been found for the lone T-28.

Once mechanical engineer Nguyen Tuan and electrical engineer Nguyen Ba Phuc had restored the aircraft's engines and electronics to working order, the Trojan was 'incorporated' into the VPAF and given the number 963 (9 for September and 63 for 1963, the month and year of Saibory's defection). Training was assigned to instructors Nguyen Van Ba and Le Tien Phuoc, while Capt Hoang Ngoc Trung, senior pilot of the

VPAF's Il-14 unit, would head the operation. The 41st Radar Company of the 291st Air Defence Regiment was to be its eyes and ears.

Lt Saibory briefly enjoyed a change of scenery from his prison cell during this period, for he flew the Trojan with Nguyen Van Ba to bring him up to strength on the type – Le Tien Phuoc and Hoang Ngoc Trung also got acquainted with the aircraft. After several flights it was evident that some engine parts needed to be replaced, as did the worn tyres, as these made further flying unsafe. Fortunately for the Vietnamese pilots, an air defence unit had shot down a T-28 in Quang Binh province, and all useable parts were salvaged by the A-33 Aircraft Repair Facility. With its 'new' parts, 963 was ready for action by January 1964.

Without proper equipment to direct operations in the air, attacks on American intruders at night could be carried out only by moonlight. The North Vietnamese tried hard to effect an interception but without success. Sometimes there was no target, or the pilot couldn't keep track of it, or if he managed to, his shots would miss.

However, their luck was about to change, for at 2330 hrs on 15 February 1964, radar units picked up an American aircraft approaching Con Cuong in Nghe An province. They tracked it flying over Truong Son, on the Ho Chi Minh Trail, heading north towards Hoi Xuan.

At 0107 hrs on 16 February, 963 received an order to scramble. Nguyen Van Ba was at the controls, and in the light of the moon he noticed a black spot against a white cloud. When he had closed to within 500 m, he fired two rounds, and the intruder, a C-123 Provider, crashed into a forest near the North Vietnam-Laos border.

Only one crewman (a member of the South Vietnamese forces) was pulled alive from the wreckage of the transport aircraft. It was the first aerial victory for the VPAF.

On 16 February 1964 Nguyen Van Ba shot down a South Vietnamese C-123 transport aircraft over the Laos-Vietnam border whilst flying this ex-Royal Laotian Air Force T-28 Trojan (*VPAF Museum*)

YEARS OF STUDY

Early in 1949, Gen Vo Nguyen Giap, head of the Ministry of Defence, Brig-Gen Hoang Van Thai, the Chief of Staff, and Phan Phac, who was in charge of military training, sought guidance from Ho Chi Minh about establishing an air force and navy. On his orders, in March 1949, they set up the Ban Nghien Cuu Khong Quan (the Air Force Research Committee), headed by Ha Dong. Its aim was to lay down the foundations of an air force by studying that of the French.

One of its first tasks was to organise courses for new recruits, and its first intake consisted of 29 pilots, ground personnel and meteorologists, whilst the second group had as many as 81 hopefuls. Training methods were gleaned from the French, and former German and Japanese prisoners-of-war taught alongside the Vietnamese.

After just a few hours of theory, the first batch of pupils, accompanied by their teachers, left their classroom for Chiem Hoa, where, in a corn field, they built a 400 m x 25 m airstrip. For lessons, just two aircraft were available – the Morane-Saulnier and the Tiger Moth. Aviation fuel was transported to the airfield from Cao Bang.

In March 1956 110 students were sent abroad for training. Eighty went to China, and of these, 50 commanded by Pham Dung began honing their skills as fighter pilots. The other 30 students, led by Dao Dinh Luyen, received instruction on Tu-2 bomber aircraft. During the course a change in priorities led to Dao Dinh Luyen taking over the fighter pilot group while Pham Dung was put in charge of the students learning on the DC-3-inspired Li-2 transport and the Mi-4 helicopter.

Three Czech-built Aero 45 aircraft were used for flight training at Gia Lam. They had arrived from China on 26 January 1956 (*VPAF Museum*)

The Soviet Union played host to a separate batch of would-be pilots, a 30-strong group of trainees learning about the Il-14 and Li-2 transports under the direction of Pham Dinh Cuong. From 1957, instruction was being given on the Il-14, Li-2, An-2 and Mi-4, and the MiG-15 was also be flown by would-be fighter pilots.

Back at home, the Vietnam Air Club (Cau Lac Bo Hang Khong Viet Nam) had been established in January 1956, and within months it had organised a trip for 12 students to Czechoslovakia to study the workings of the two-seat Zlin-226 Trener 6 sport aircraft. Their new-found knowledge was soon put to good use, and they were sent to Cat Bi airfield, where Vietnam's defence chiefs had set up the Civil Aviation Department Flying Club, and with it the first official home-based training unit for the country's air force, the No 1 Training School (Truong Hang Khong So 1). They were joined by 13 newly-qualified instructors who had been taught on the Yak-18 in China, as well as five Czech instructors and some Chinese advisors.

Recruits were taught the skills of their particular fields, whether meteorology, signals or engineering. The unit was supplied with eight Trener 6 aircraft from Czechoslovakia and a similar number of Yak-18 (CJ-6) aircraft from China in April 1959.

No 2 Training School (Truong Hang Khong So 2) was established at Gia Lam, where radio operators and mechanical engineers were trained. The unit used three Czech-made Aero 45s, which had been delivered from China in January 1956.

The first groups of pilots returning home from China at the end of their three-year training stint soon began to share their skills with others. Early in 1959 they were assigned to training flights on Il-14, An-2, Li-2 and Mi-4 aircraft, and played their part in helping to create a transport section on a proper regimental level. On the first day of May the 919th Air Transport Regiment (Trung Doan Khong Quan Van Tai 919) was formed at Gia Lam, and within months the 910th Training Regiment (Trung Doan Khong Quan 910) and Air Force Training School (Truong Khong Quan Viet Nam) were up and running.

The principal trainer for the 910th was the Yak-18. By 6 October 1959 the first 12 students had clocked up 20 hours on the type, and were

North Vietnamese trainee pilots that were sent to China received their first taste of flying in piston-engined Yak-18 basic trainers. Just 13 pilots from this initial group of students succeeded in gaining their wings, and they returned from China to North Vietnam in April 1959 to become instructors at Cat Bi (*VPAF Museum*)

11

transferred to the 919th Air Transport Regiment for advanced training on the Il-14, Li-2 and An-2 types. The following year, 87 students joined the course at Cat Bi.

Some 52 pilots who had done their time on the Yak-18 now found they would get the chance to try out a different beast, and in 1960 were sent to China for conversion to the MiG-17. By then the first batch of North Vietnamese airmen trained on the MiG-15 by the Chinese had arrived home, and a detachment of 31 qualified flyers was taken to the Chinese base at Son Dong for conversion onto the MiG-17. They and about 200 technicians were later moved to Mong Tu, near the North Vietnamese border, so they could get home quickly if the need arose.

By the end of 1962 the first pilots to finish their courses on the MiG-17 in the Soviet Union and China returned to Vietnam. Moscow decided that a gift to mark the achievement was required, and it sent 36 MiG-17 fighters and MiG-15UTI two-seat trainers to Hanoi on 3 February 1964. With these the 921st 'Sao Do' Fighter Regiment was established.

North Vietnamese student pilots discuss their next training exercise in front of a J-5 (MiG-17) at Mong Tu air base in China (*VPAF Museum*)

Dang Ngoc Ngu (above the cockpit) and his fellow classmate listen to Russian instructor A M Yuriev as he describes the controls of a MiG-17 at an air base in the Soviet Union (*via István Toperczer*)

North Vietnam's defence chiefs realised that the advantages of a trained air force went beyond fixed-wing aircraft, and planned to establish a helicopter regiment too. A group of 67 pilots were duly sent off to the Soviet Union for helicopter conversion. They finished their course in 1964, but a shortage of aircraft meant there was no regiment for them to join.

Aside from flying the MiG-15UTI, North Vietnamese pilots also used the Chinese-built two-seat version of the MiG-17, the JJ-5 (*VPAF Museum*)

In the wake of the Tonkin Gulf Incident in the first week of August 1964, the Americans extended the air war north of the border into communist Vietnam. Defence ministry officials and air force chiefs decided to call the 921st Fighter Regiment home from China, and on 6 August the Regiment's pilots landed at Noi Bai airfield. During their first four months back on home soil, they flew far more hours than in an entire year in China, being constantly in the air training other pilots. When not flying, they would be practicing in their 'hi-tech simulators' – cockpits made from bamboo that had been set up in front of their living quarters.

In the summer of 1965 another 30 fighter pilots returned from Krasnodar, in the Soviet Union, and from China, doubling the number of available flyers. The VPAF quickly made use of them, for on 7 September a second fighter regiment – the 923rd 'Yen The' – was formed. The 923rd would be equipped with the MiG-17, whilst the 921st now operated both MiG-17s and MiG-21 fighters.

By June of the following year Hanoi's MiG-17 pilots had completed their studies in the Soviet Union, and come November 1966, a further 18 pilots had graduated on the type. Sixty per cent of them would have experienced combat by the end of the year.

In 1967 two-thirds of those trained on the MiG-17 were assigned to the MiG-21, boosting the numbers flying the latter type. In January 1968, 14 MiG-17 pilots graduated from courses with the 910th Training Regiment and were immediately posted to join their fighter colleagues at the 921st and 923rd.

In February 1969, the Ministry of Defence decided on a new addition. The 925th Fighter Regiment was to be formed at Yen Bai airfield and equipped with MiG-17F and J-6 (the Chinese version of the MiG-19) fighters. The unit's members would be recruited from among the MiG-21 pilots who had studied in the Soviet Union, and from MiG-17 graduates put through their paces by the 910th Training Regiment on home territory.

The pilots practised in flights of four, eight or twelve aircraft, in bad weather and also at night. Within two months the 925th had nine MiG-19 and four MiG-17 pilots sufficiently qualified for combat duty.

Although the number of trained pilots was increasing, their level of combat experience against the Americans varied widely. At the 919th Air Transport Regiment, meanwhile, training was progressing, with both adverse weather and night-time bombing practice against land and sea targets.

Before long another sympathetic communist nation was to provide its skills to the North Vietnamese cause – Cuba. In 1971, on the orders of Vietnam's Chiefs of Staff and the VPAF high command, ten MiG-17 pilots were selected from the 923rd to prepare for ground attack missions. Under a cooperation agreement between Hanoi and Havana, a Cuban pilot and some technical staff were sent to help devise tactics for attacking American warships. By March 1972, the 923rd could boast six pilots from its ranks qualified to attack targets at sea.

By this time the American people were weary with war. President Richard Nixon ordered his generals to win it, and in one final push Vietnam's air defences took a hammering. Operation *Linebacker II* involved B-52 bombers flying 3000 sorties, and dropping about 40,000 tons of explosive. But within a short time American involvement in the long years of debilitating conflict was over.

All the VPAF's training aircraft were destroyed during the *Linebacker* offensive, forcing training units to move to China. These schools, as well as the Aircraft Repair Facility, were then put under the direct supervision of the VPAF high command, and towards the end of 1973 training restarted, although the number of aircraft available was limited – ten pilots had to share one aircraft. MiG-17 training flights were conducted by the 923rd Fighter Regiment at Kien An, Tho Xuan, Vinh and Dong Hoi, and the programme was helped when the 925th was given 24 MiG-19s by China in 1974.

The weather was often bad over Yen Bai air base, making things tough for the novices, and lessons were frequently disrupted. Half the pilots in the 921st and 927th had little flying experience, and apart from those flying patrols, all the 'old hands' had to muck in training the new recruits. By the end of 1974 the rookies had graduated.

On 22 February 1974, an agreement was signed between the North Vietnamese and Chinese air forces, promising Chinese assistance in founding a Vietnamese People's Air Force Academy and a maintenance factory for the MiG-17. Under the terms of the deal, China would help expand the Kien An base, where the academy would be built. Basic flight training would be provided for 50 pilots a year, 30 of whom would be sent to fly fighters, and up to 300 technical personnel would also pass through the academy. China would also help rebuild and expand the aircraft maintenance workshops, which would have the capacity to repair 50 fighters a year.

UNDER THE RED STAR

MiG-17s and MiG-21s were the aircraft that most Vietnamese pilots trained on in the Soviet Union. The Krasnodar Flight Officers' School, situated between the Black Sea and the Azov Sea, had four airfields assigned to it – Bataysk, Primorsko-Ahtarsk, Kushchovskaya and Krasnodar. Vietnamese, Hungarian and Cuban cadets being grouped in separate squadrons, although they jointly participated in theory classes and flight training. There were also students from other countries, such as Afghanistan, Albania, Iraq, Cambodia, Laos, Mongolia and Syria, but they were far fewer in number.

Vietnamese students looked forward to their training, although the Russians only allowed them to participate in the final stages of the

КАБИНА ЛЕТЧИКА

Vietnamese pilots made use of this custom-built cockpit trainer during their conversion onto the MiG-17 'Fresco-A' in the USSR (*József Vanyó*)

Student pilots practise retracting and extending the landing gear of a 'jacked up' Yak-18 'Max' at Bataysk airfield in the early 1960s (*Tibor Hajdú*)

syllabus once they had been deemed fit both physically and mentally, on the ground and during evaluation flights. The drop-out rate was high – sometimes only 20 out of 100 students would make it as pilots, with the rest becoming ground technicians. Compare these figures with the record of the Hungarian students – from the 38 who started flight training in 1962, 35 graduated as pilots come the end of the course in the summer of 1965.

However, it has to be said that most of the Hungarians already had a basic knowledge of flying thanks to being members of aviation sports clubs, while for many of the Vietnamese this was the first time they had ever seen an aircraft! Not surprisingly, perhaps, the Russian instructors jostled to be allocated with the Hungarian students, while trying to avoid the Vietnamese. On the other hand, training for the Vietnamese was shorter and faster, and because of the war became even more intense from the mid-1960s.

Following a Russian language pre-school, training began in the autumn of 1960 with close to 20 theoretical subjects – aircraft, propulsion system, structure, flight theory, radio-electronics, on-board equipment, meteorology, map-reading, tactics and so on. The autumn and winter months were taken up with theory and other ground training, while spring and summer were ideal for actual flying.

In April 1961 training began on the Yak-18A at the Bataysk grass

A Russian instructor demonstrates the correct take-off technique to his pupils through the use of a model of a MiG-15. After landing, the brakes of the MiG-15UTI would become extremely hot, so fire brigade personnel would usually sprinkle the tyres with water (*Zoltán Pintér*)

Besides the MiG-17 'Fresco A', the MiG-15UTI 'Midget' was also a principal training tool for would-be VPAF fighter pilots under instruction at Kushchovskaya. Students flew in excess 80 hours on the MiG-15UTI, followed by a further 100 hours at the controls of the MiG-17 (*István Karancz*)

strip near Rostov, continuing from September at Kushchovskaya (nicknamed 'Kushcho') on the MiG-15UTI and MiG-17 'Fresco A' until the end of 1962 – cadets flew 100 hours on the Yak-18 and 150 on the MiG. 'Kushcho' had a concrete runway, which was used for take-offs, but landings were made on the adjacent grass strip to save the tyres. Flight training for the Vietnamese was almost always conducted from 0600 hrs until 1230 hrs, when cumulus clouds usually started forming.

Students flew during daylight hours only, and the Vietnamese had an advantage over the others when training time was allocated. Still, they needed about twice as many hours as the others before they went solo for the first time.

Among the problems they encountered was the change-over from the Yak-18 to the MiG fighter. An example of the troubles encountered by the Vietnamese pilots was recounted to the author many years later by a Hungarian fighter pilot who had been a cadet undergoing fast jet conversion at the time. He had asked his Russian instructor how the Vietnamese were progressing with their training, and the latter replied, 'if five Vietnamese pilots take off in MiG-17s on a routine flight, twelve Russian pilots have to sortie in order to collect them from the sky!'

Several mishaps occurred during the course of their training. Sometimes the VPAF pilots overshot the runway – 'they went grazing', as the Russian instructors would say – and several aircraft were damaged whilst being taxied back to the apron due to over-eager manoeuvring. Hungarian and Cuban students would be 'sentenced' to a week's ground training if they transgressed, but the Vietnamese were allowed to fly the following day due to the urgency with which they were required back home.

Flight training consisted of simple aerobatics, route flying, easy dogfights, air-to-air sorties against static targets and attacks on ground targets, but only in good weather. Firing with live ammunition was carried out once or twice a year with the MiG-15UTI or MiG-17, either in solo or dual, with 30 rounds for each cannon.

Parachuting and ejector-seat training were also part of the curriculum. Twice a year students hurled themselves from An-2 aircraft, and an annual

ground ejection seat ride on the simulator, fired by an explosive charge, was also completed. Sometimes training was spiced up, and an example of this occurred at Biryuchy (the diversion airfield for 'Kushcho'), where the head of the parachute operation put on a show with a live ejection from a modified MiG-15UTI which was missing its rear canopy.

Each year a day-long medical was held for students at Krasnodar. The Vietnamese had a healthy life-style, for unlike the others, they did not smoke, drink or court Russian women! In their spare time they practised marshal arts in the gym and, despite, the Russians' attempts to persuade them against it, studied the teachings of Mao. The Vietnamese always had a greater respect for China than for the Soviet Union, and back in Vietnam a graduate from the Chinese Military Academy would command the utmost respect.

The class of 1962 attended lessons in theory in Bataysk, but primary training on the Yak-18 was conducted from Primorsko-Ahtarsk (nicknamed 'Ahtari'). The following year they too took flights on the MiG-15UTI and MiG-17 from Kushcho.

This period gave rise to various stories, but there is one in particular that has been told time and again. A Russian instructor was preparing for a circuit of the airfield with a Vietnamese student. All the flight details and manoeuvres had been rehearsed using a model aircraft over a map of the airfield painted on the tarmac. Running through this theory, the Vietnamese student didn't put a foot wrong. Once airborne in the MiG-15UTI, the student performed his first turn then climbed to 1500 m instead of the compulsory 500 m. The instructor told him to check the altitude. 'Immediately, Comrade Captain', came the reply, but he made no correction.

Soon the instructor pushed the control column forward, which resulted in a 1000 m drop before the aircraft levelled off at 500 m. He again told the student to carry on and check the altitude. The puzzled Vietnamese replied, 'Comrade Captain, the altitude is still 500 m!' He had failed to notice that following take-off the small hand on the altimeter had already made a full circle and was standing on 1000 m, while he was concentrating exclusively on the large hand on the 500 m mark!

Joking aside, both the successes and failures of the Vietnamese pilots who were passing through the course were later used by Russian instructors as examples when they taught successive classes.

A Vietnamese student is seen practising his close formation flying for the benefit of the camera during a sortie from 'Kushcho' in MiG-17 'Fresco-A' 'Blue 61' in August 1964 (*Sándor Legoza*)

During the first six months of 1962, several cadets arrived at Krasnodar for conversion to the MiG-21. Vietnamese students had struggled with the subsonic MiG-17, and the supersonic MiG-21, with its high landing speed, proved quite a challenge to them. The ideal student would be 18 to 20 years old, taller than average, and of stronger physical build. However, a typical Vietnamese pilot was small in stature and light in weight, placing him below the minimum weight for the aircraft's ejector seat, and making the fighter's controls difficult to operate. This resulted in VPAF pilots experiencing real problems in physically flying the aircraft, which occasionally proved fatal.

The HUD (Head-Up Display) was above their line of sight, and their legs could barely reach the rudder pedals. Nor did they possess the physical stamina required for the type. When pulling between five and seven Gs, they had trouble with their vision and experienced dizziness, leading some instructors to install a mirror in the front cockpit so they could see when students fainted due to high G-loads.

Despite such physical handicaps, most VPAF students managed to overcome these problems, even with the introduction of the MiG-21 which brought with it still more tactical taskings. Indeed, ground targets were now expected to be attacked as well, and pilots had to practise bombing runs and firing unguided missiles from the UB-16-57 launcher.

In 1966 there were several changes to the training syllabus. At 'Ahtari', the Yak-18 was abandoned in favour of the Czech-built L-29 Delfin jet trainer. Students had to complete 80 hours on the type before moving on to Kushchovskaya for the MiG-15UTI and MiG-17, where a further 40 hours on each type was logged. Prior to finishing the course in the first half of 1968, the students returned to Krasnodar to complete 40 hours on MiG-21PFM and MiG-21US trainers. This particular course was also the first VPAF group to tackle night training, with pilots completing between eight and ten hours on the L-29, ten to twelve hours on the MiG-17 and eight to ten on the MiG-21.

Some of the North Vietnamese pilots who joined the course had already completed flight training on the MiG-17 in China, so for them, once they had dealt with the L-29, it was straight into the cockpit of the MiG-21. Out of the original 40 students, 20 successfully completed the type conversion course, but within six months eight had lost their lives in combat over Vietnam.

From 1966 Vietnamese students received their first taste of fast jet flying in the Czech-built L-29 Delfin. Pilots would fly 80 hours on this type, including ten at night (*Zoltán Pintér*)

A North Vietnamese student pilot was killed in the crash of this L-29 at 'Ahtari' in the early 1970s. He was conducting his first solo flight in the Delfin at the time, and during his approach to land he thought there was a problem with the jet's undercarriage. He panicked, stalled the L-29 and plummeted into a housing estate in Primorsko-Ahtarsk (*Zoltán Pintér*)

Some accidents happened on Delfins as well, which was hardly surprising, since the Vietnamese had to undergo a more advanced training programme on these new jets, involving aerobatics, stalling and spinning. There were emergency landings without an engine, or with an engine on fire. In one case a student on his first solo was completing a basic circuit when he thought there was something wrong with his undercarriage. He panicked and stalled the L-29, plunging to his death into a block of flats in Primorsko-Ahtarsk.

The practice of using the L-29/MiG-17/MiG-21 combination in training continued into the early 1970s, although there were fewer Vietnamese students on the courses. With the intensity of the air war over Vietnam in 1972, the units back home needed all the help they could get, and it was not until 1974 – a year or so after the signing of the Paris peace treaty – that larger groups of VPAF pilots once again arrived in the Soviet Union for basic and advanced training.

The Russians supplied a small number of surplus L-29s to the VPAF from 1971 onwards, these machines being used in-country to train pilots destined to fly fast jets (*via István Toperczer*)

SILVER SWALLOWS

In June 1963 a top-level decision was made to amalgamate the VPAF and the Air Defence Forces. The new entity, the Air Defence Forces-Vietnamese People's Air Force (Phong Khong - Khong Quan Nhan Dan Viet Nam) emerged on 22 October 1963 under the command of Col-Gen Phung The Tai. His deputy was Col-Gen Dang Tinh.

The ADF-VPAF combined the air defence units, radar units and the air force under one command. The air defence forces consisted of 11 regiments, of which three were dedicated to radar units, with 18 companies looking after radar equipment. The VPAF at the time had a transport wing (the 919th) and a training wing (the 910th). It controlled ten operational bases, with a few others under construction, and had 83 aircraft on strength – 44 transports, 12 helicopters and 27 trainers.

As the war got underway, the North Vietnamese had to build up their air force and air defences from a standing start in a very short time. They had few fighters, and were hugely outnumbered by US Air Force and Navy fast jets. In addition, the standard of training for fighter pilots was far inferior to that of their opponents.

The problems for the ADF-VPAF was further complicated by the shape of the country, which made defence against fast-flying attackers almost impossible. North to south, North Vietnam stretches for 800 kms, but is very thin, with a width of just 70 kms in the south and 400 kms in the north. There was often little warning of US jets coming in from various directions, and the attackers were usually over their targets within minutes of crossing into the coast. By the time the fighters were scrambled, they were already too late – the intruders had been and gone.

With almost 60 per cent of the country covered by jungle, further headaches were created for units trying to transport radar equipment. And the radar itself had its drawbacks. Coverage up to a height of 500 m-1000 m worked for a maximum distance of 40 kms, whilst continuous operation above the 500 m level was possible only over flat areas such as the coastline and in the Red River valley. Conversely, in other parts of the country the radar worked only above 4000 m.

Part of the job of detecting low-flying intruders fell to observers, and look-out posts were set up. Using radio, they were able to report on

These MiG-17s were part of the first batch of 36 'Frescos' supplied to the VPAF by the Soviet Union. Issued to the 921st Fighter Regiment, the aircraft were flown into Noi Bai airfield from China on 6 August 1964 (*via István Toperczer*)

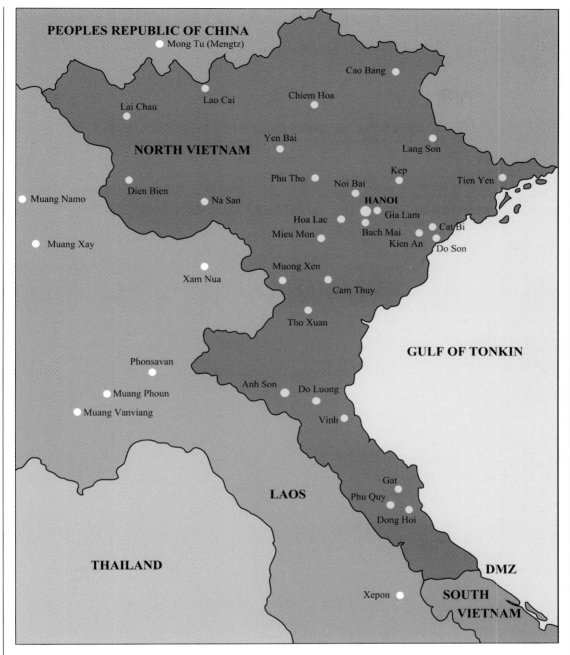

PEOPLES REPUBLIC OF CHINA

Mong Tu (Mengtz)

Cao Bang

Chiem Hoa

Lao Cai

Lai Chau

Yen Bai

NORTH VIETNAM

Lang Son

Kep

Phu Tho   Noi Bai   Tien Yen

Muang Namo

Dien Bien   Na San   HANOI

Gia Lam

Hoa Lac   Cat Bi

Mieu Mon   Bach Mai

Muang Xay   Kien An

Do Son

Muong Xen

Xam Nua

Cam Thuy

Tho Xuan

GULF OF TONKIN

Phonsavan

Anh Son

Muang Phoun   Do Luong

Muang Vanviang   Vinh

LAOS

Gat

Phu Quy

Dong Hoi

THAILAND   DMZ

Xepon   SOUTH

VIETNAM

incoming American pilots, but the system was by no means foolproof, for the number of observation posts was limited, and a vast number of US aircraft were never detected. In 1966 the weakest link in the Vietnamese air defences was still its early-warning radar capability, and the lack of proper communication with fighter units. At this time, the ADF-VPAF high command had control over radar units and equipment directly responsible for the protection of important industrial and municipal centres. They had no authority at all, however, over those belonging to military districts and regional defence committees.

This map reveals the location of all the major airfields from which the VPAF operated during the conflict in Vietnam. Airfields in neighbouring Laos and China are also marked

The problems for the fighter units were compounded by the fact that the air defence system operated only periodically. Without proper direction from the ground, pilots in most cases had to find their targets purely with their eyes. This did have its advantages though, for larger formations of enemy aircraft – say perhaps between eight and ten – could be seen from up to 15 kms away in daylight. Without radar to alert the American pilots to the fact that they had been spotted, the North Vietnamese could sneak up on the fighter-bombers undetected.

The Vietnamese had only a limited amount of airspace in which to engage their foes, for they were forbidden to enter areas protected by AAA units, or those guarded by SAM sites, unless they were returning home at an altitude of 500-600 m. Indeed, coordinated action by fighters and SAM units within the same defence area was rare. In special cases, such as in a pursuit, or if a pilot was finishing an attack, braking off from a dogfight or preparing to land, he would be given permission by the command centre to operate at a different altitude.

The risk of 'friendly-fire' incidents was high. In 1966 alone, defence units opened fire on their own airmen on ten occasions, shooting down two MiG-21s and badly damaging the others.

As the war dragged on, a continuous supply from China, the Soviet Union and other communist countries provided a sufficient amount of hardware. There were fighters (MiG-17/F/PF, MiG-19, MiG-21F-13/PF/PFM/MF), radar units (P-12 'Spoon Rest', P-15 'Flat Face', P-35 'Bar Lock' and PRV-11 'Side Net'), surface-to-air missiles (SA-2, SA-3, SA-7, SON-4/9, 'Fan Song' and 'Low Blow') and conventional anti-aircraft artillery weapons (37, 57, 85 and 100 mm).

And with an ongoing training programme for pilots and ground units, the air defences became increasingly effective both day and night.

BUILDING THE BASES

The war against France ended in 1954, with the People's Army of Vietnam (PAVN) having fought a successful campaign equipped in the most part with weaponry seized from surrendering Japanese forces in the wake of World War 2! On 10 October that same year Vietnamese forces moved into Hanoi, the 308th Brigade of the PAVN occupying Gia Lam airfield. The 367th Regiment was quickly formed to operate and maintain the base, while the French agreed to carry out ground control duties. Defence chiefs appointed Nguyen Van Giao as director, while Tran Quy Hai was named as commanding officer.

When the Airfield Research Committee was established, its main function was to operate existing air bases, and to help the General Staff build an air force. Dang Tinh was

The 'Song Ma' Regiment's P-15 'Flat Face' early-warning radar could detect targets up to 250 km away at a minimum altitude of 300 m. The P-15 was mounted on a ZIL-157K 6x6 truck, which gave it cross-country mobility. Forty 'Flat Faces' were put into operation in North Vietnam (*Tran Dinh Kiem*)

The SA-2 'Guideline' (designated the S-75 Dvina by the Soviets) was a medium to high-altitude surface-to-air missile system that proved highly effective against non-manoeuvring targets such as aircraft on bombing runs (*Gábor Pálfai*)

The North Vietnamese first used the SA-3 'Goa' (Soviet-designation S-125 Neva) low to medium-altitude SAM system for protecting their airfields in late 1972 (*VNA*)

These MiG-17Fs were photographed (by an undisclosed American reconnaissance aircraft) in their earth-walled revetments under the hillside that overlooked Kien An (*via István Toperczer*)

appointed to head the committee in May 1955, and one of its roles was to carry out the necessary repairs at damaged airfields in order to make them operational once again.

Three airfields in particular had important strategic value in North Vietnam – Cat Bi, Kien An and Do Son (of these, only Cat Bi was a military base). Towards the end of 1955, work commenced on the extension of the runways and reconstruction of facilities at Gia Lam and Cat Bi, with the latter becoming the overflow base for Gia Lam. The airfields at Vinh, Dong Hoi, Lang Son, Lao Cai and Tien Yen were also rebuilt.

By 1957, the committee had looked at 42 airfields in the north, 12 of which were situated on plains, 11 in hill ranges and 19 in the mountains. Two more sites – Do Son and Cao Bang – soon became operational.

The following March the committee was told by Hanoi to get the Na San and Dien Bien airfields in the north-west military district repaired before December. The task was finished by 20 November, despite the workforce being equipped with little more than primitive tools. As part of the reconstruction came new facilities such as warehouses, repair shops, control centres and meteorological offices. By the beginning of 1959 the north had a network of airfields.

South of Hanoi was Gia Lam, Vinh and Dong Hoi, to the north-west Na San, Dien Bien, Lai Chau and Lao Cai, in the north-east Cat Bi, Kien An, Do Son and Tien Yen, and in the north Lang Son and Cao Bang.

The building of Noi Bai (Phuc Yen) airfield began on 1 May 1960, and due to the sheer scale of the project, the Vietnamese turned to Chinese engineers to provide much needed technical expertise. Construction of the base consumed 100,000 tons of cement, 200,000 tons of steel, 200,000 cubic metres of wood, 2000 tons of bitumen, 150,000 tons of petrol and 200,000 cubic metres of sand. In an area close to 1000 hectares in size, three million cubic metres of earth was moved, around 250,000-260,000 cubic metres of concrete was mixed for the runways and 150,000 cubic metres of concrete was poured for

Eleven Shenyang J-5s and a solitary JJ-5 two-seat trainer sit neatly lined up at an unnamed base prior to the commencement of the US campaign against VPAF airfields. All North Vietnamese MiGs wore four-digit tactical 'Bort' numbers, applied in red, on the nose. The first digit referred to the batch number with which the aircraft arrived in North Vietnam, whilst the second and fourth numbers were the radio call sign of the individual aircraft. The first four jets in this line-up are painted light grey overall, and have clearly had their original Chinese insignias forward of the tailplane crudely airbrushed out (*VPAF Museum*)

the aprons. The workforce required for this size of scheme was vast too, with more than 10,000 people working each day as 200 trucks delivered the materials. By mid-1964 the important parts of the base were in place, allowing the first MiG-17s to fly in from China.

FIRST AIR BATTLES

On 3 February 1964, Lt Gen Hoang Van Thai, deputy Minister of Defence, signed order 18/QD to establish the 921st 'Sao Do' Fighter Regiment (Trung Doan Khong Quan Tiem Kich 921) under the command of Lt Col Dao Dinh Luyen. Brig-Gen Tran Quy Hai, the deputy Chief of Staff, presented the unit's flag, known as the 'Invincible Flag'.

In response to the American campaigns (OPLAN 34A, *DeSoto* and OPLAN 37-64), the ADF-VPAF was placed on full alert in March 1964. OPLAN 34-A had been approved in January 1964 by President Lyndon B Johnson, and it called for a 12-month programme of covert actions. Notably, OPLAN 34-A included the use of US Navy destroyers to perform coastal reconnaissance (codenamed *DeSoto* patrols) in the Gulf of Tonkin, with one or more aircraft carriers from the Seventh Fleet steaming close by to provide assistance if needed. South Vietnamese gunboats were also cleared to shell targets in the North Vietnamese panhandle.

In response, Ho Chi Minh gave the order, 'Those who intrude into the Northern air space must be shot down'. By the summer the situation had become increasingly tense, following 202 intrusions in the first six months. On orders from President Johnson, the number of aircraft carriers in the South China Sea was steadily increased.

On 1 June PAVN Chief of Staff, Brig-Gen Van Tien Dung, ordered that the entire army be put on alert.

Two month later, on 2 August, the destroyer USS *Maddox* (DD-731) came under attack from North Vietnamese torpedo boats while operating in territorial waters, and apparently assisting a covert South Vietnamese commando raid. This, and a reputedly fictitious second attack by torpedo boats two days later, resulted in Operation *Pierce Arrow*, a reprisal air raid on 5 August.

Pierce Arrow had been authorised by President Johnson in the wake of the Tonkin Gulf incident, the first wave of sorties being launched in the early afternoon of 5 August as soon as USS *Constellation* (CVA-64) joined USS *Ticonderoga* (CVA-14) in the Tonkin Gulf. Both air wings flew a combined total of 67 sorties against North Vietnamese patrol boat bases at Hon Gai, Loc Chao and Quang Khe, destroying eight boats and damaging a further twenty-five. The petroleum-oil storage tanks at Vinh city were also struck, with the 90 per cent of the facility being destroyed. Two aircraft (both from the *Constellation*) were lost to AAA during the operation, A-1H BuNo 139760 from VA-145 (its pilot, Lt(jg) R C Sather, was killed) and A-4C BuNo 149578 from VA-144 (pilot Lt(jg) Everett Alvarez was made a prisoner of war).

Following this dramatic escalation in hostilities, the North Vietnamese decided it was time to call their fighters home from China. Van Tien Dung was in charge of the secret 'X-1' project, and the pilots involved were briefed in China about *Pierce Arrow* by Lt Col Nguyen Van Tien, second-in-command of the VPAF.

On the morning of 6 August, a valedictory ceremony was held at Mong Tu that saw a North Vietnamese flag hoisted on the control tower. Groundcrews carried out final checks on the line of aircraft while the pilots awaited take-off. At Noi Bai it was sunny, but the sky over southern China was overcast until noon. When the weather cleared, flares shot into the air and flights of four MiG-17 'Fresco-As' began to roar into the sky, heading south-east. Wing Cdr Dao Dinh Luyen (1), Pham Ngoc Lan (2), Tao Minh (3) and Lam Van Lich (4) took off first, followed by three more four-strong formations of MiG-17s.

Later at Noi Bai, Van Tien Dung, along with the commander of the VPAF, Phung The Tai, and his deputy, Dang Tinh, were present when Pham Ngoc Lan became the first pilot to land a MiG fighter on North Vietnamese soil. Once all the 921st Fighter Regiment's aircraft had landed, each pilot was personally congratulated. The date of 6 August 1964 became a landmark in North Vietnam's history – the nation had a brand new air arm.

Later that same day, the VPAF placed the first two pairs of alert aircraft (MiG-17s) on stand-by to be ready to scramble for real, with Pham Ngoc Lan and wingman Lam Van Lich in the first flight, and Tran Hanh with wingman Nguyen Nhat Chieu in the second. Despite the fanfare greeting the arrival of the 921st, ADF-VPAF commanders were fully aware that their air force was still far from ready to fight the USAF and US Navy. It had few trained pilots and few aircraft in comparison with the more technologically advanced, and well-trained, American contingent.

This North Vietnamese MiG-17 'Fresco-A' still wore Cyrillic stencilling below the cockpit when it was photographed in the late summer of 1964. The jet is fitted with the early-style ejection seat which lacked a face curtain (*Zoltán Pintér*)

Following the arrival of the *'én bac'* ('Silver Swallows', as the jets were affectionately known by the Vietnamese), air force chiefs discussed plans on how to succeed in the first aerial engagement. A handful of young, inexperienced pilots would be flying obsolete aircraft against a numerically and technically superior enemy. They had one advantage though. They would be flying over their own territory, with back-up, however limited, from radar and anti-aircraft units.

Pilots regularly discussed their ideas about air combat tactics among themselves. One enthusiast recommended suicide attacks if necessary by ramming enemy aircraft. Although this dedication and willingness for self-sacrifice was greatly admired, the idea of kamikaze-style *taran* (ramming), as the Russians called it, did not find any takers among the upper echelons. They preferred tactics that would ensure victory with the smallest possible loss.

Le Trong Long, who had served in a commando unit before joining the air force, suggested surprise attacks similar to commando assaults. Tran Hanh explained how he would evade cannon fire, and Lam Van Lich expounded on how to avoid being caught from behind. Le Minh Huan discussed the capabilities of American air-to-air missiles.

In an effort to give their pilots a better understanding of the enemy, air force commanders regularly grilled captured US air crew for information, although the success of these sessions was limited due to the PoWs misleading their captors with false information. Photographs of American aircraft were also closely studied so that pilots could identify them more easily. After a while, VPAF tactics started to take shape.

Following much analysis, senior air force officers came to the conclusion that the Americans had an Achilles Heel. US pilots would fly in with predetermined objectives, with large numbers of aircraft following routes which would rarely alter. Many would be heavily laden with bombs, compromising their agility. In all, this made them vulnerable.

MiG-17 pilots believed their mounts were capable of fighting at the same altitude as the intruders, and that their guns would be effective at close range – they planned to lure the Americans into dogfights. To get a kill on their first pass, they practised firing from 300 m down to 150 m.

Pilots were carefully selected for each flight. Air force commanders knew that a few were destined to become aces, but 'team players' were equally as important. Skill, experience, character and personality were all taken into account. Capt Tran Hanh, who almost seemed able to make a MiG-17 'talk', became a flight leader. His wingman, Pham Giay, was quiet, studious and helpful. Numbers three and four in the flight were Le Minh Huan and Tran Nguyen Nam, who had been born in neighbouring provinces, and were close friends. 1Lt Pham Ngoc Lan, who was also an outstanding pilot, led another flight, with the less skilled, but highly disciplined, Phan Van Tuc on his wing. Ho Van Quy, the flight's number three, was a good navigator, whilst Tran Minh Phuong, flying as number four, had a flair for air-to-air shooting.

On 11 November 1964, Ho Chi Minh visited the 921st Fighter Regiment. With him were high-ranking party and government leaders like Le Duan, First Secretary of the Central Committee, and Truong Chinh, President of the National Assembly. Such visits were made not just to inspect the units, but to fire up the pilots with enthusiasm, for the

On 5 August 1964, Lt(jg) Everett Alvarez (pilot of A-4C BuNo 149578 from VA-144, embarked on the USS *Constellation*) became the first naval airman captured by the North Vietnamese after his Skyhawk was downed by AAA during the *Pierce Arrow* raid. He subsequently spent almost nine years in captivity (*Vietnamese Embassy, Budapest*)

Dao Dinh Luyen was the first fighter wing commander of the VPAF. In March 1956 he led the first group of 30 Vietnamese which started bomber pilot training on the World War 2-vintage Tu-2 in China, but was soon reassigned to the group learning to be fighter pilots. On 3 February 1964 Luyen was selected to be the commander of the 921st Fighter Regiment, and on 6 August he led the first flight of VPAF MiG-17s home from China. Attaining the rank of colonel, Luyen was eventually promoted to air force commander-in-chief in May 1977 (*Tran Dinh Kiem*)

The 921st's Capt Lam Van Lich familiarises himself with the new ejection seat, fitted with a face curtain and stabilising panels, recently installed in this MiG-17. He is wearing a MiG-15-style leather helmet and goggles over a textile cap. On 3 February 1966 Capt Lich was credited with the first VPAF night kill in a jet, flying a MiG-17PF (*Vietnamese Embassy, Budapest*)

Airfield gun crews get training in precision shooting with the help of a of small wooden model of an F-105D Thunderchief (*Gábor Pálfai*)

speeches of 'Bac Ho' ('Uncle Ho') would motivate the audience. At one stage he told them;

'The Vietnamese way of warfare is distinctive. Even a rudimentary weapon becomes effective in the hands of the Vietnamese. We should exploit it, and should not fear that the enemy has much more modern weaponry'.

Prior to the first aerial engagement taking place, a conference was called where everyone agreed that, from the very first air battle, the North Vietnamese had to win. They also agreed that they would attack only if the Americans crossed the 20th Parallel at Thanh Hoa.

Following the start of the American *Flaming Dart I-II* and *Rolling Thunder* campaigns, the VPAF high command decided on 2 April 1965 that two flights would take part in the first counter-offensive. Pham Ngoc Lan remembers;

'My flight consisted of Phan Van Tuc (my wingman), Ho Van Quy and Tran Minh Phuong, while the second flight was made up of Tran Hanh and Pham Giay.

'The weather was foggy over Noi Bai air base on the morning of 3 April, with visibility of between four and five kilometres and 6/10ths cloud with a base of 300 m. Over the anticipated battle area the volume of cloud was 5-6/10ths, with the cloud base up to 700 m and visibility of up to ten kilometres. At 0700 hrs, the radar operators reported a group of intruding fighters in North Vietnamese airspace, which left after carrying out their reconnaissance duties. The North Vietnamese command felt that a large formation would subsequently attack the bridge at Ham Rong following this earlier flight. Col-Gen Phung The Tai once again briefed the pilots on their objectives, and ordered a stage-one alert. As anticipated, at 0940 hrs US aeroplanes attacked the bridges at Tao, Do Len and Ham Rong.

'At 0947 hrs the second flight was launched from Noi Bai. As the leader of the first attack flight, I took off at 0948 and followed a heading of 210° towards the province of Thanh Hoa. Our flight closed to within 45 kms of the intruders at 1008 hrs, while the second flight was still flying over

This VPAF-ADF GAZ BTR-40 scout vehicle has been fitted with a 20 mm AAA mounting. The design of the Russian-built BTR-40 was heavily influenced by the American M3A1, 3340 examples of which were suppled to the USSR during World War 2. The vehicle is seen moving to a new site near Noi Bai airfield in September 1967 (*Gábor Pálfai*)

Myriad M38/39 37 mm automatic AAA guns like this one protected Kep and Yen Bai airfields. The gun's effective range was three kilometres, and it was easily transported behind a ubiquitous ZIL-151 or -157K 6x6 truck (*Tran Dinh Kiem*)

The 57 mm, S-60-towed, AAA gun was issued predominantly to anti-aircraft regiments tasked with defending North Vietnamese airfields (*Gábor Pálfai*)

Ninh Binh Province. I informed air control at 1009 hrs that we had made visual contact with the intruders, and they responded with an order to drop our external fuel tanks and engage the enemy.

'The bridge at Ham Rong was attacked in pairs by the American fighter bombers, who were at this time still unaware of our fighters. My wingman and I quickly latched on to the tails of two American fighters, and when in range I opened fire with my cannons, and the F-8 Crusader in front of me exploded in a ball of fire and crashed. I was later credited with the first American fighter-bomber to be shot down by a North Vietnamese fighter pilot.

'At the same time the aircraft of Ho Van Quy and Tran Minh Phuong were also pursuing another pair of intruders, with the latter pilot flying as wingman. Ho Van Quy opened fire, but the Americans were out of range and both jets managed to escape, although the battle between the MiG-17s and the F-8 Crusaders was still far from over in the area of Ham Rong. At 1015 hrs my wingman, Phan Van Tuc, reported on the radio that he had spotted an American fighter to his right, and I immediately replied with an order to attack as I in turn became his wingman. He succeeded in closing in on the American and opened fire with his cannons, eventually causing the F-8 to crash.

'At 1017 hrs Phan Van Tuc, Ho Van Quy and Tran Minh Phuong received an order to land and they duly returned home. In the meantime, I was running out of fuel in the vicinity of our airfield, and ground control gave me the order to eject. However, I thought that there was still a chance to save the aircraft, which was of considerable value to the VPAF, and still had many more battles left in it! I looked for a suitable landing ground, and spotted a long sandy strip on the bank of the Duong River, on which I made a successful landing.'

Once Lan's gun camera film had been developed, the image of a blazing F-8 was perfectly visible. However, according to official US sources, all

four F-8Es (from VF-211, off USS *Hancock* (CVA-19)) recovered from the encounter, although the jet flown by Lt Cdr Spence Thomas was so badly damaged that he had to land ashore at Da Nang. The only official loss for the navy on this mission was A-4C BuNo 148557, flown by VA-216's Lt Cdr R A Vohden. Downed by AAA, the pilot spent the rest of the war as a PoW.

Although it now appears that the MiG pilots failed to score any kills on their debut mission, the original goal of the VPAF had nevertheless been fulfilled – that enemy aircraft had been successfully engaged during this first encounter. Commemorating the engagement, 3 April would subsequently be recognised as Air Forces' Day by the Vietnamese people.

On the evening of 3 April, the commanders of the 921st gathered for a meeting to evaluate their success, and make plans for further encounters. They felt that both the pilots and the regiment as a whole had been properly prepared, and that this was the main reason for their success. The pilots had been able to use the element of surprise, and in the heat of battle had stuck to the basic tactics of shooting down as many intruders as possible, while protecting their own aircraft, engaging only in close dogfights and concentrating their force against a single group of intruders.

Other lessons were also learned from mistakes made during this encounter. Some pilots had fired when out of range, wasting valuable ammunition – more than 680 rounds were fired, of which 160 consisted of 37 mm shells, and 526 of 23 mm.

Meanwhile, the commanders felt that since the Americans had failed to destroy the bridge at Ham Rong, they would be back the following day to bomb it once again. And if the unit could time its attack correctly, the enemy would be surprised yet again.

It was decided that if the Americans did mount another strike on the Ham Rong bridge, its first line of defence would be provided by the AAA sites that had enjoyed success the previous day. The fighters would only attack after the gunners on the ground had finished firing. Once given the order to take-off, the 921st would initially put up a decoy flight that would head west at an altitude of between 7000 and 8000 m.

Meanwhile, the attack flight would be patrolling at a lower altitude on a south-east heading, climbing only when approaching the enemy to gain a height advantage. The operation would be led by the regiment's second-in-command, Nguyen Van Tien, while ground control would be in the hands of Dao Ngoc Ngu.

The 921st's Pham Ngoc Lan and Phan Van Tuc participated in the first Vietnamese-US dogfight of the war on 3 April 1965 when they intercepted two F-8 Crusaders over Ham Rong (*VNA*)

On the morning of 4 April the Americans made several reconnaissance flights over Thanh Hoa which were to precede an attack on Ham Rong bridge and the power plant at Thanh Hoa. At 1020 hrs the Vietnamese decoy flight (consisting of pilots Le Trong Long, Phan Van Tuc, Ho Van Quy and Tran Minh Phuong) took off. They climbed to 8000 m and flew over Vu Ban and Phu Ly, in Nam Ha Province, in an attempt to attract the attackers' attention. Tran Hanh takes up the story;

'As the leader of the attack flight, made up of Pham Giay, Le Minh Huan and Tran Nguyen Nam, I took off at 1022 hrs. The weather was very cloudy, with considerable fog patches. My flight received orders from ground control to descend to low altitude and head east, then, again on orders, changed the heading to south-east. As my flight approached the area of the anticipated interception, we quickly gathered altitude to gain advantage. I reported at 1030 hrs that we had visual contact with the Americans. I had spotted a group of four F-105Ds which had just started dropping their bombs, and I ordered my wingman, Pham Giay, to cover me in the attack.

'At a distance of 400 m, I opened up with all three cannons, downing one of the F-105s which fell in flames into the sea. The Americans turned to attack us, and we split into two groups. My wingman and I stayed on the southern side of the Ham Rong bridge, whilst Le Minh Huan and Tran Nguyen Nam flew across to the northern side. Supported by Tran Nguyen Nam, Le Minh Huan downed another F-105D. In the ensuing combat, the numerical superiority of the Americans resulted in the loss of my wingman, as well as Le Minh Huan and Tran Nguyen Nam.

Tran Hanh and Pham Ngoc Lan examine gun camera film beside a MiG-17 for the benefit of the photographer. Pham Ngoc Lan completed his flying training in China, and was the first VPAF pilot to land at a North Vietnamese airfield in a jet aircraft. Lt Lan became a flight leader in the 921st Fighter Regiment, and was the first VPAF pilot credited with shooing down a US military aircraft. Later, he was selected for conversion onto the MiG-21, and in April 1975 he oversaw the training of MiG-17 pilots tasked with flying captured Cessna A-37B Dragonfly light attack aircraft. Pham Ngoc Lan is seen here wearing an SL-60 (summer issue) leather helmet and khaki flying suit (*Vietnamese Embassy, Budapest*)

'Indeed, I was only able to escape through hard manoeuvring, but I lost contact with ground control in the process. Short on fuel, I had to land at the first possible opportunity, and I successfully put my MiG down in Ke Tam valley (Nghe An Province), but was immediately arrested by the locals – I was only able to regain my freedom after showing them my VPAF badge. I was taken to the provincial capital, where the commander turned out to be my friend with whom I had fought against the French in the 320th Army Division. After bidding my host farewell, I returned to my unit.'

In this second engagement, the VPAF pilots had not enjoyed the same element of surprise as they had done 24 hours earlier. Yet the encounter had shown that even though the air force was in its infancy, and not so well equipped, it could still be successful in the air. The three MiGs that were lost during the course of the action were reportedly shot down by the F-105s according to sole survivor Tran Hanh, although USAF records indicate that no kill claims were made by any of the returning pilots – perhaps the VPAF pilots fell victim to 'friendly' flak.

The USAF did confirm the destruction of two F-105Ds (59-1754 and 59-1764) from the 355th TFW on this day, however, pilots Maj F E Bennett and Capt J A Magnusson both being killed in action.

On 5 April Defence Minister Vo Nguyen Giap and PAVN Chief of Staff Van Tien Dung were extensively briefed on the previous days' clashes when they visited the 921st Fighter Regiment. Ho Chi Minh sent a telegram to the air force, which read;

'You have fought bravely and shot down the American aeroplanes, and you are worthy of the traditions of our people and army. I am congratulating you, but at the same time asking you to further improve your fighting spirit against the American aggressors. Don't be conceited with your victories, and do not let yourself be stopped by difficulties on the way.'

In the summer of 1965 things took a turn for the worse, as the still-maturing fighter force was decimated. Losses were blamed on the lack of combat experience, inferior hardware and over-zealous air defence units. Furthermore, in the wake of the first encounters with the MiGs, Lockheed EC-121D Warning Star airborne early warning and fighter control aircraft were deployed to South Vietnam to conduct missions off the coast of North Vietnam in an attempt to prevent surprise attacks.

The VPAF also suffered from a high accident rate. As an example of the latter, on 17 June Nho Quan, in Ninh Binh Province, was the scene of a large aerial combat between four MiG-17s and twenty A-1H Skyraiders and F-4Bs from USS *Midway* (CVA-41). The VPAF claimed two Phantom IIs destroyed (none were lost according to official navy records),

North Vietnamese pilots and ground personnel discuss the latest mission behind a MiG-17 'Fresco-A' at Noi Bai in 1965. Other canvas-covered MiG-17s can be seen parked in the distance (*VPAF Museum*)

At 1053 hrs on 4 April 1965, Tran Hanh shot down F-105D 59-1754 of the 355th TFW in the immediate vicinity of Ham Rong bridge. The pilot of the Thunderchief, Maj F E Bennett, was killed in the engagement (*VPAF Museum*)

Tran Hanh was leading a formation of four MiG-17s on 4 April, the remaining pilots being (from left to right) Pham Giay, Le Minh Huan, and Tran Nguyen Nam. Aside from Tran Hanh's victory, Le Minh Huan also downed F-105D 59-1764 – again its pilot, Capt J A Magnusson, failed to eject from his Thunderchief. The VPAF also suffered losses during this engagement, for Pham Giay, Le Minh Huan and Tran Nguyen Nam were all killed. Mysteriously, the surviving 355th TFW pilots did not claim any MiG kills upon returning to their base at Takhli, in Thailand, so perhaps the trio of young Vietnamese pilots fell victim to 'friendly' flak (*via István Toperczer*)

but in turn had two MiG-17s shot down by AIM-7 Sparrow missiles fired from a pair of F-4Bs from VF-21. A third MiG crashed into a mountain, killing its pilot. A similar accident occurred three days later, when two MiG-17s caught six Skyraiders over Mai Chau, in Hoa Binh Province.

The Vietnamese flight leader fired seven times before he claimed to have hit his target. His wingman also reported a kill, but a low-altitude manoeuvre in turn saw him fly into a mountain. Again, no A-1Hs were lost by the navy on this day, the unit involved (VA-25, again off the *Midway*) turning the tables by claiming credit for the MiG that had crashed.

On 20 July two MiG-17 pilots reported shooting down an F-4 Phantom II at Tam Dao, in Vinh Phu Province, but later both MiGs were destroyed by the Americans with the loss of both pilots. Once again there were no confirmed losses for either the US Navy or USAF on this date, and no MiG kills claimed either, so it appears as if either 'friendly' flak or an accident claimed the VPAF jets. Ten days earlier, however, on 10 July, two MiG-17s were claimed (with AIM-9 Sidewinder missiles) by two F-4C crews from the 45th TFS/15th TFW. On this occasion it was the turn of the VPAF to record no combat losses!

Despite these erroneous victory claims and counter-claims, the VPAF had nonetheless discovered that whenever their pilots did actually manage to shoot an American aircraft down, they too suffered losses. Staff at VPAF headquarters tried to work out why this was occurring, and found that some of the tactics being employed were less than effective. For instance, instead of attacking heavily-laden strike aircraft, pilots would regularly tangle with escort fighters. And because of the early 'successes' enjoyed by the 921st in April, some flight leaders subsequently held their enemy in contempt, having been lulled into a false sense of security. The VPAF command duly ordered units to take part in fewer engagements.

In May 1965 Vice-Premier Le Thanh Nghi ordered the defence chiefs to expand the airfields at Hoa Lac, Yen Bai, Tho Xuan and Kep, whilst the airfields at Gia Lam and Kien An had to be totally rebuilt. The work on the latter bases was duly completed by year-end.

Kep had to be ready sooner, however, in preparation for the arrival of the newly-formed 923rd Fighter Regiment. To hit the schedule, all the workers at the Bac Giang fertiliser factory were requisitioned and housed by the residents of Lang Giang. The railway authorities laid on a special service, and other workers came from the army. Soon, there were no fewer than 4000 people getting the airfield ready, using 700 cubic metres of

concrete a day and removing a total of 500,000 cubic metres of earth from the base. The work was meant to take eight months, but this was considered too long by the Ministry of Defence, who decided to speed things up by levelling surrounding hills with dynamite! The 2nd Pontoneer Brigade of the 3rd Military District, advised by experts from the Technical University, sank several hundred shafts into the hills, and about 250 tons of explosive was placed in them and detonated on 8 July. Then the building teams moved in. Among their tasks was the diversion of a river that provided irrigation for neighbouring fields by digging a new channel away from the airfield. The final metres of runway were laid towards the end of August.

On 7 September the base was ready, and the 923rd 'Yen The' Fighter Regiment (Trung Doan Khong Quan Tiem Kich 923), under the command of Maj Nguyen Phuc Trach, was formed specifically to fly from the new facility. By the end of 1965 work at the remaing four sites had also been completed, giving North Vietnam a brand new airfield network.

In late 1965 MiG-21F-13s and MiG-17PFs arrived from the Soviet Union, allowing both fighter wings to be reorganised with two squadrons in each. The 921st Fighter Regiment was based at Noi Bai and the 923rd at Kep, the former unit being equipped with MiG-17s and MiG-21s, and the latter exclusively with MiG-17s. In addition to the new aircraft, the VPAF's capability was drastically improved through the introduction of ground-based P-35 and PRV-11 radar units.

From the summer of 1965, US fighter-bombers concentrated on destroying roads and railway lines in the Lang Son, Lao Cai and Hai Phong provinces near Hanoi and in the 4th Military District (which was centred around Vinh city, in the southern region of North Vietnam).

Following a two-month lull, from September, North Vietnamese pilots were back in the air.

The primary north-south supply line, dubbed 'Route 1' by the Americans, was attacked on the 20th of that month between Lang Son and Hanoi. A flight of four MiG-17Fs from the 921st was scrambled from Noi Bai to meet the intruders, and Pham Ngoc Lan recounts the action;

'I was the leader of the flight, accompanied by Nguyen Nhat Chieu, Tran Van Tri and Nguyen Ngoc Do, and as we climbed we spotted the American aircraft flying over Yen Tu at 3000 m. We were ordered to drop our wing tanks, accelerate and attack. We immediately turned right and attacked a flight of four US Navy F-4s.

'The Phantom pilots had not noticed us until it was too late. Two F-4s pulled hard up while the other pair broke to starboard. Not intending to get into a vertical fight, we stayed with the turning Phantoms. One of them was attempting to disappear into a cloud, while his wingman made a dive towards the earth. My wingman, Nguyen Nhat Chieu, was in an

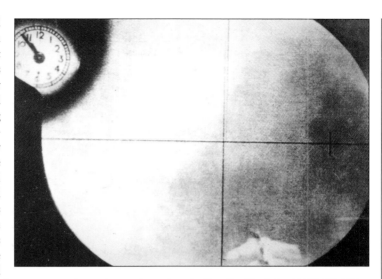

Tran Hanh's victim, F-105D 59-1754, is clearly visible in this frame from the VPAF pilot's gun camera film (*VPAF Museum*)

Le Minh Huan's victim (F-105D 59-1764) is seen plunging earthwards just minutes after Tran Hanh had downed a Thunderchief. The pilot of this machine, Capt J A Magnusson, failed to eject and was killed when the fighter-bomber hit the ground. Moments later Le Minh Huan was also dead, his MiG-17 almost certainly having been struck by 'friendly' AAA (*VPAF Museum*)

ideal position to follow the former, which started to turn left into the cloud.

'The Phantom's predictable flight path allowed my wingman to take a short cut and close in on him. Popping out of the cloud, the Phantom headed for the sea with Nguyen Nhat Chieu on his tail, opening fire when he was within 400 m. Trailing black smoke, the

F-4 began a slow descent and tried to escape, only to receive another burst from the MiG's trio of cannon. The Phantom crashed into a mountain near Nha Ham in Ha Bac Province. Our flight returned home safely'.

Once again there is no official US Navy Phantom II combat loss for 20 September 1965. Sixteen days later, on 6 October, an F-4B crew from VF-151 (off the USS *Coral Sea* (CVA-43)) claimed a MiG-17 with a Sparrow missile – the kill does not match VPAF loss records. On the 14th of the month a MiG-17 pilot *was* credited with a victory over an F-105D of the 36th TFS/6441st TFW (pilot, Capt R H Shuler, was killed), although the confirmation came from the USAF rather than the VPAF! Indeed, the pilot responsible for this victory never actually made a claim.

The final aerial kill of 1965 that can be confirmed by both sides occurred on 6 November, when a MiG-17 flight from the 921st Fighter Regiment, comprising Tran Hanh, Ngo Doan Hung, Pham Ngoc Lan and Tran Van Phuong, 'bounced' a US helicopter (a CH-3C combat rescue and recovery machine) over Hoa Binh.

From 3 April 1965 to December of that year, VPAF aircraft had been scrambled 156 times, and marked up 15 kills. The aerial battles proved that the subsonic MiG-17s could effectively tackle the superior F-105 and F-4 fighters, and at low altitude, where neither American type was as manoeuvrable as the Russian fighter, the MiG-17 had a considerable advantage – this was due primarily to high external weapon loads, according to captured US pilots.

A MiG-17 'Fresco-A' is towed away from the flightline by a Chinese copy of the Soviet ZIL-157K 6x6 truck – note the 12.7 mm machine gun mounted just behind the cab. The Chinese Shenyang Aircraft Factory began the production of MiG-17F fighters under the designation J-5 (or F-5) in 1955 with Soviet assistance. Early examples were assembled mainly from Soviet-made parts, while from 1956 all the components, including the engines, were manufactured by the Chinese. The VPAF generally did not differentiate the MiG-17Fs of Soviet and Chinese origin. Thus, aircraft described as MiG-17Fs could be either the original Soviet product or a Chinese-manufactured Shenyang J-5 (*VPAF Museum*)

Le Trong Long (below left) claimed this US Navy F-4B Phantom II (off the *Midway*) destroyed during a dogfight over Nho Quan on 17 June 1965. Navy loss records fail to confirm Long's kill, however (*via István Toperczer*)

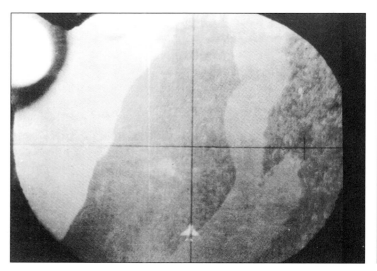

Kep air base was declared operational on 7 September 1965. As this aerial view of one of the airfield's numerous dispersal areas clearly shows, there were separate shelters for individual MiG-17s away from the main runway – which is out of shot (*via István Toperczer*)

There was another factor which played into the hands of the VPAF when dealing with the F-105 in particular. Typically, the pilot of the Thunderchief would be concentrating on the accurate delivery of his bombs, rather than looking exclusively for fighters. F-4 crews were also at a distinct disadvantage in these early dogfights, as their aircraft's primary air-to-air weapons were guided missiles, which required an optimum launch range to work effectively. The MiG-17, of course, relied on good old-fashioned cannon, which proved vastly superior to often unreliable missiles during a close-in engagement.

Yet despite these advantages, Vietnamese pilots often returned to base without having scored any kills, and this was due primarily to the poor standard of their training. For example, pilots had trouble in maintaining the necessary battle formation, VPAF MiG-17s being sent into combat almost entirely in flights of four. Initially, the MiG-17 pilots flew tight formations, with just 50-100 m separation between lead and wingman, and 100-200 m between the two pairs. This may have been good for formation display flying but not for combat, as it required the pilots to concentrate too much on each other in order to maintain position, rather than keeping a look-out of the enemy.

Other tactical disadvantages stemmed from the lack of opportunity to show individual initiative. Learning from these early losses, the VPAF spread the formations to 600-800 m between aircraft and 800-1200 m between the pairs. Later, the flights became even more spaced, with 2000 m horizontal and 400-500 m vertical separation between the pairs.

PATROLS

In February 1966, after a lull in fighting that lasted from 24 December to 31 January, the Johnson administration ordered the resumption of aerial bombing of North Vietnam. At the same time, Hanoi instructed the VPAF to protect important transport infrastructure, and to attack enemy installations and transport.

On 3 February, Lam Van Lich from the 921st Fighter Regiment was credited with the VPAF's first night kill with a jet aircraft. Flying a MiG-17PF, he claimed two A-1H Skyraiders destroyed over Cho Ben, in Hoa Binh Province – no such losses appear in official US records.

The first MiG-17PF 'Fresco-Ds' arrived in North Vietnam at the end of 1965 from the Soviet Union – VPAF records indicate that only ten 'Fresco-Ds' were supplied to the Vietnamese. The diaelectric panels on the jet's nose housed the two antennas of the RP-5 Izumrud 'Scan Rod' fixed-scan ranging radar. This system worked on the two-antenna principle, with one used to search for targets and the other used for tracking them once acquired. Instead of the N-37D cannon of the standard MiG-17F, the PF was equipped with a third NR-23 cannon (*VPAF Museum*)

The P-35 'Bar Lock' early-warning radar had a range of 300 km and an accuracy of plus or minus 900 m. Antennae and radar equipment was fully mobile, being transported on a purpose-built two-axle trailer (*Tran Dinh Kiem Collection*)

Another 'first' occurred on 4 March, when the 923rd Fighter Regiment made its combat debut with the MiG-17. Phan Thanh Chung, Ngo Duc Mai, Tran Minh Phuong and Nguyen The Hon had taken off at 1542 hrs on a patrol of the Yen Bai-Phu Tho region, and at 1600 hrs they ran into US aircraft. Phan Thanh Chung opened fire, but was unable to get a hit, whilst Ngo Duc Mai got within 500 m of a Phantom II before it broke away prioring to firing on it. He persevered, however, and this time closed the distance to 200 m and hit the F-4 with a number of rounds. The American jet 'shuddered and exploded' – no combat losses were reported by either the USAF or US Navy on this date.

After the fight, the airmen headed home, and were preparing to land when they saw that the Americans had followed them. Ngo Duc Mai turned around to challenge the Phantom IIs, but the enemy reportedly broke off the engagement. Mai was now running very low on fuel, and at 1620 hrs he was forced to make an emergency landing.

On 26 April, the 923rd Fighter Regiment's Ho Van Quy downed two F-4Cs and damaged a third over Bac Son-Binh Gia, in Lang Son Province. USAF records note no losses to fighters on this day, and in turn credit its crews with the destruction of five MiG-17s and one MiG-21 during the month of April. Ironically, the only aircraft lost to Vietnamese fighters – a solitary USAF A-1E, reputedly downed by a MiG-17 on 29 April – was not claimed by the VPAF!

By the summer, American forces were regularly attacking Hanoi, Hai Phong and other military and industrial centres, the air battles beginning in earnest on 4 June. During the course of ten engagements, twelve US aircraft were claimed by VPAF fighters, and 24 hours later two pairs of MiG-17s destroyed two F-8s – the Vietnamese pilots all returned safely home. Two more Crusaders were downed on 21 June over Kep by MiG-17s flown by Phan Thanh Trung, Duong Trung Tan, Nguyen Van Bay and Phan Van Tuc.

Again, according to USAF and US Navy records, the only loss attributed to VPAF fighters in June was F-8E BuNo 149152 of VF-211, flown by Lt Cdr Cole Black (who remained a PoW until 1973), which was downed on the 21st. His squadronmates avenged his loss by claiming a total of four MiG-17s on 12 and 21 June. An RF-8A lost on this day was also claimed by the VPAF, although navy loss records state that it fell to AAA.

On 29 June, the USAF struck fuel dumps at Duc Giang, in Hanoi, and at Thuong Ly, in Hai Phong. To counter the raids, the 923rd sent up four MiG-17s. Tran Huyen, Vo Van Man, Nguyen Van Bay and Phan Van Tuc tackled a group of 12 F-105 Thunderchiefs and downed two of them over Tam Dao – the solitary jet officially listed as missing was credited to AAA by the USAF. In return, the 388th TFW was awarded the F-105's first official MiG-17 kill of the conflict.

Phan Than Trung from the 923rd claimed a kill against an unidentified enemy aircraft on 13 July over An Thi, whilst the US Navy also credited the crew of an F-4B from VF-161 (aboard the *Constellation*) with a single MiG-17 victory. The following day – again in the vicinity of An Thi – Ngo Duc Mai downed F-8E BuNo 150908, flown by VF-162's CO, Cdr Dick Bellinger. The American succeeded in ejecting from his crippled jet, and was quickly returned to the USS *Oriskany* (CVA-34). Bellinger later downed a MiG-21 on 9 October 1966.

On 17 July Le Quang Trung and Ngo Duc Mai claimed the 1200th and 1201st US aircraft destroyed over North Vietnam, their A-4s being 'downed' near Hung Yen – no Skyhawks were reported as having been lost by the US Navy on this date.

Two days later twelve F-105s from the 354th TFS/355th TFW were detected flying over Tam Dao at an altitude of between 600 m and 1500 m, heading for Noi Bai airfield, north of Hanoi. Armed exclusively with missiles, the aircraft appeared to be on a 'MiG-hunting' mission. Nguyen Bien and Vo Van Man of the 923rd were ordered to attack, being given instructions not to open fire until they had closed to within 600 m of the American fighter-bombers. At 1450 hrs the two MiG-17 pilots took off, and they soon ran into two pairs of F-105s some 1500 m apart.

The Vietnamese pilots increased speed, and a steep climb brought them in behind one of the American fighter-bombers. Nguyen Bien opened fire from 600 m, but the USAF pilot had spotted him and got out of the way. Getting behind the MiG, he in turn tried to shoot it down with numerous bursts of cannon fire, but missed. A furious dogfight developed with the arrival of the remaining F-105s, and the MiG pilots decided to lure their enemy into the flak belt that surrounded Noi Bai.

East of the base, Vo Van Man abruptly turned and got behind an F-105. He duly hit the USAF jet (F-105D 59-1755) with two well-aimed bursts and it crashed, killing its pilot, 1Lt Steven Diamond. Keen to avenge the loss of their comrade, the remaining American pilots

Capt Tranh Hanh climbs down from a MiG-17PF radar-equipped all-weather interceptor to the applause of the assembled groundcrew. Hanh was one of the first pilots to complete fighter training in China. Considered to have exceptional aeronautical skill, he became a flight leader immediately upon the 921st Fighter Regiment's return to North Vietnam in August 1964. Following service as Dao Dinh Luyen's deputy, Hanh was promoted to command the 921st in early 1966. Eleven years later he was selected as Deputy Commander in Chief of the VPAF. Here, Hanh is wearing a standard-issue brown leather flying jacket and green nylon PPK-1 anti-G webbing over a green textile flying suit and black leather shoes (*Vietnamese Embassy, Budapest*)

attempted to press home their numerical advantage but were continually thwarted by the fierce flak barrage. Two minutes after Diamond had crashed to his death, a second Thunderchief was claimed by Nguyen Bien, while a third F-105 was reportedly hit by flak and exploded over Tuyen Quang. The USAF only officially acknowledge the loss of two F-105s on this sortie, the second having reportedly been downed by AAA. Both MiG-17s recovered safely at Gia Lam airfield in Hanoi

The second half of 1966 saw a whole series of aerial engagements fought out over North Vietnam, giving the MiG pilots plenty of opportunity to put into practise their anti air-to-air missile tactics. These often proved very effective – for example, in September, a MiG-17 pilot was returning to his base when two F-4s succeeded in getting within missile distance. Launching a number of AIM-7 rounds from between 1500-2000 m, the American crews were foiled in their attempt to down the VPAF fighter thanks to a series of well-rehearsed evasive manoeuvres flown by the MiG pilot.

The more effective, but shorter-ranged, AIM-9 Sidewinder could also be defeated if spotted early enough, and with the missile trailing smoke and flame once launched, visual acquisition was not usually a problem. The VPAF pilot would immediately start flying a snaking pattern with his jet, the basic manoeuvre calling for him to turn his MiG-17 at a 70° angle of bank, and pull between three and four Gs towards the incoming missile at a speed of 700-900 km/h. In most cases this manoeuvre was enough to shake off the missile's heat-seeking lock-on system, which homed in on the jet's exhaust.

These MiGs show signs of having their previous national insignias painted over, the new VPAF markings being applied over crudely-sprayed patches. This would suggest that they are ex-Chinese Shenyang J-5s rather than Soviet-built MiG-17Fs. All four jets are being prepared for an imminent launch (*VPAF Museum*)

A 921st Fighter Regiment MiG-17PF 'Fresco-D' undergoes a pre-flight check on 3 February 1966. That night Lam Van Lich claimed to have shot down two A-1H Skyraiders (*via István Toperczer*)

Technicians complete their final checks on Ngo Duc Mai's MiG-17. He was credited with the first aerial victory for the 923rd, on 4 March 1966, when he claimed a Phantom II over Phu Tho – this kill is not substantiated by official US combat records (*VPAF Museum*)

Phan Van Tuc and Nguyen Van Bay claimed the destruction of two F-105Ds over Tam Dao on 29 June 1966, with Tuc's victim being captured on his gun camera film. USAF records, however, state that just one Thunderchief (60-0460) was lost, and that this machine (flown by the 388th TFW's Capt Murphey N Jones, who became a PoW) was shot down by AAA (*via István Toperczer*)

If the MiG was flying at an altitude higher than 800 m, and the basic turn did not shake off the Sidewinder, the pilot would use a more elaborate method. By increasing the angle of bank, he slowly started to dive. The pilot had not pushed the control column forward, however, which meant that he could carry on constantly changing the direction of the aircraft in different planes. This manoeuvre was similar to a spiral in its early stage, although in this instance the pilot was performing a slow descending roll. The simultaneous movement of the aircraft both in vertical and horizontal planes was usually enough to free the MiG from missile lock.

Between June and December of that year, MiG-17 pilots claimed 18 US aircraft destroyed, although American sources confirm exactly half of this number. During the same period, USAF crews were credited with six MiG-17 and three MiG-21 victories, whilst their US Navy equivalents downed six MiG-17s, one MiG-21 and two An-2 transports.

One of those aircraft confirmed by the Americans as having been destroyed by VPAF fighters was a single F-8E (of two claimed) from VF-111. Flown from the *Oriskany* by USAF exchange pilot Capt W K Abbott, BuNo 150896 was downed on 5 September by an unnamed MiG pilot. Abbott spent the rest of the war as a PoW.

Sixteen days later USAF F-4C Phantom IIs from the 433rd TFS/8th TFW were intercepted by two pairs of MiG-17s. The leader of the first pair enjoyed an altitude advantage going into the engagement, and he opened fire from 500 m, closing to 200 m. His rounds struck home, and F-4C 63-7642 was shot down – pilot Capt R G Kellems and Weapon Systems Officer (WSO) 1Lt J W Thomas ejected, and were subsequently recovered by a USAF Combat Search and Rescue team.

On 2 December Noi Bai air base was attacked yet again by USAF F-4s and F-105s from an altitude of 2000-2500 m. MiG-21s and MiG-17s were scrambled in advance of the strike, with the former type operating above 2000 m and the latter below this altitude. The MiG-21 pilots were instructed to engage the American aircraft as they commenced their bombing runs, while the MiG-17s were to attack when the fighter-bombers pulled out of their dives.

The first engagement took place between a pair of MiG-17s and two F-105s as they attempted to egress from the target after dropping their bombs. The MiG wingman opened fire first on the trailing F-105, but he was too far away to achieve a hit – the Thunderchief pilot engaged afterburner and disappeared.

The leading MiG pilot then attacked, and he also fired at too great a distance. The lead F-105 pilot tried to shake him off, but his afterburner failed to ignite and his evasive manoeuvring allowed the MiG-17 to get within firing distance. The VPAF pilot opened fire from 150-200 m, downing the Thunderchief with three bursts. The USAF fail to list any F-105s lost to VPAF fighter activity on this day, although on 5 December F-105D 62-4331 of the 421st TFS/388th TFW was destroyed by a MiG-17, and its pilot, Maj B N Begley, posted Missing in Action (MIA) – official VPAF records do not list this kill.

On 17 July 1966, at Hung Yen, Le Quang Trung and Ngo Duc Mai claimed the 1200th and 1201st US aircraft (two A-4s) shot down over North Vietnam. No Skyhawks were lost in combat on this day according to US Navy records
(*via István Toperczer*)

These same records do state, however, that during 1966, 55 per cent of all enemy aircraft lost over North Vietnam fell to VPAF fighters. Specifically, in 196 aerial engagements fought that year, the Americans lost 54 aircraft – 36 of them to MiG-17s. US records, on the other hand, note that just 12 aircraft were downed by communist fighters, as many as ten of which fell to the MiG-17.

With their growing combat experience, the VPAF's fighter regiments were officially credited with having repelled 1991 raids on the Hanoi region alone. Pilots had also got considerably better at making the most of their ammunition. For example, in 1965 a MiG-17 pilot had typically used 65 rounds of 37 mm and 247 rounds of 23 mm ammunition to achieve a kill, yet by the end of 1966 that figure had fallen to an average of 43 of the former and 150 of the latter.

On 19 July 1966, the 923rd's Nguyen Bien (below) shot down F-105D 60-5382 of the 354th TFS/355th TFW over Vinh Phu, killing its pilot, 1Lt Steven Diamond. USAF records state that the Thunderchief was hit by 57/85 mm AAA, but Bien's gun camera film clearly shows the F-105 being hit by cannon rounds fired from his MiG-17F
(*via István Toperczer*)

Despite the VPAF's kill claims being drastically overstated, the modest force of MiG pilots had nonetheless achieved great things in less than two years of combat, and they were honoured in a ceremony held in Hanoi in December 1966. Medals were presented to the 1st Squadron of the 921st Fighter Regiment and to the 2nd Squadron of the 923rd. They were also awarded to Tran Hanh, Nguyen Van Bay and Lam Van Lich.

OVER HANOI AND HAI PHONG

The Americans continued to attack power plants, industrial sites, major routes and military installations around Hanoi and Hai Phong during the dry season of 1966-67, the USAF and US Navy attempting to cut off Hanoi from Hai Phong, and in the same way isolate the two cities from other areas. Air defence positions in Viet Tri, Thai Nguyen and Quang Ninh provinces were also attacked. Vietnamese defence chiefs also expected the bombing of water processing plants and weirs along the banks of the Red River, whilst on-going attacks against air bases continued to hamper the operational capabilities of the VPAF.

In an effort to make the best use of its handful of fighters, the air force concentrated on defending Hanoi itself. And although the VPAF's effectiveness had been greatly enhanced by the arrival of MiG-21s, the backbone of the fighter force was provided by the tried and tested MiG-17s. The combined use of the two types, employing their capabilities to the full, was regarded as vitally important by the VPAF's high command. However, the MiG-21 force was decimated by Col Robin Olds' 8th TFW in the first week of January (nine were claimed to have been destroyed in two engagements – on the 2nd and 6th – by the F-4C-equipped wing), and the type was temporarily withdrawn.

The first MiG-17 kill listed by the VPAF for 1967 occurred on 5 February over Luong Son, in Hoa Binh province, when an unidentified pilot claimed an F-4 Phantom II – no matching loss can be found in US records. On 26 March the 921st Fighter Regiment was also credited with having destroyed an F-4C over Hoa Lac, in Ha Tay province, although USAF records state that this machine was downed by AAA.

The MiG-17 pilots did inflict corroborated losses on 19 April, however, when an F-105F (63-8341, of the 357th TFS/355th TFW), crewed by Majs T M Maddison and T J Sterling, and an A-1E (52-133905, of the 602nd ACS/432nd ACW), flown by Maj J S Hamilton, were downed over Suoi Rut, in Hoa Binh province. The Thunderchief crew were captured and the A-1 pilot posted MIA. The VPAF claimed two F-105s and two A-1s (an E- and a H-model) on this day.

The USAF, in turn, stated that the F-105s had downed four MiG-17s during the engagement on the 19th, following on from the three credited to the fighter type

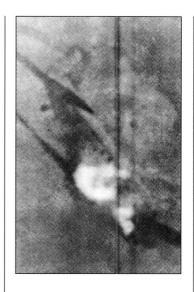

On 29 July 1966, Luu Huy Chao of the 923rd Fighter Regiment shot down USAF RC-47D 43-48388 of the 606th Air Commando Squadron, which was on an electronic and photographic reconnaissance mission over Hoa Binh. Capts R E Hoskinson and B Conklin, and their crew, were reported as missing in action (*via István Toperczer*)

MiG-17s overfly a busy ramp at the 921st's Noi Bai home in 1966. The overall 'natural metal' MiG-17 'Fresco-A' fighters all wear red tactical numbers on their noses. Such line-up shots would become a thing of the past once the Americans started targeting VPAF airfields (*VPAF Museum*)

in March. Both the Thunderchief and the Phantom II would continue to inflict heavy losses on the VPAF as the year wore on.

A few weeks prior to the 19 April action, Vietnamese Defence Minister Vo Nguyen Giap supplied the ADF-VPAF with missile and radar units that had recently arrived from the USSR and China. He simultaneously changed the VPAF's structure, creating the 371st 'Thang Long' Air Division (Su Doan Khong Quan 371) to control the 921st and 923rd fighter regiments, as well as the 919th Air Transport Regiment. The airfields at Gia Lam, Noi Bai, Kep, Hoa Lac, Kien An, Tho Xuan and Vinh were also assigned to the 371st. By this stage of the war, the air force had 64 fighter pilots, 1685 technicians and 1024 ground controllers.

The new division was headed by Lt Col Nguyen Van Tien, with Lt Cols Hoang Ngoc Dieu and Dao Dinh Luyen as his vice-commanders. Lt Col Tran Manh and Lt Col Nguyen Phuc Trach were also promoted to joint second-in-command of the fighter regiments.

The VPAF's main role was still to defend Hanoi and the system of dykes around the Red River. The Vietnamese fighters did not always respond to every intrusion into the north due to the small number of available pilots, choosing instead to oppose strikes on important targets.

On 23 April Kien An airfield, near Hai Phong, was hit from the air, the raid causing severe damage both to the runway and surrounding buildings. However, within 36 hours the airfield was operational once again, thanks to civilian and military personnel from Truong Son and Thai Son.

Hanoi was attacked by 24 enemy aircraft the following day, and two MiG-17 flights from the 923rd Fighter Regiment responded. The first, comprising Vo Van Man, Nguyen Ba Dich, Nguyen Van Bay and Nguyen The Hon, claimed two F-4s, while the second flight of Mai Duc Toai, Luu Huy Chao and Hoang Van Ky were credited with destroying a third Phantom II. These were navy jets from *Kitty Hawk's* VF-114, and one F-4B (BuNo 153000) was indeed lost, although US records state that it fell to AAA. The fighter's crew, Lt Charles Southwick and Ens James Laing (who both became PoWs), had themselves claimed a MiG-17 (with an AIM-9D) just moments earlier, as had their squadronmates Lt Denny Wisely and Lt(jg) Gareth Anderson (who used an AIM-9D).

VPAF air bases – escpecially the ones which could operate MiGs – were high-priority targets of the US bombing campaign. Thanks to the assistance of the civil population living nearby, the airfields were usually restored to operational status within 24 hours of the attack taking place. The defusing and removal of unexploded bombs, such as this high-drag Snakeye, was done by specialists, however (*VPAF Museum*)

One of the flights involved in this large-scale action on 24 April had employed new low-level ambush tactics recently devised by the VPAF. Ordered into the air by the Chief Command, four MiG-17s from the 923rd (flown by Nguyen Van Bay, Nguyen The Hon, Ha Bon and Nguyen Ba Dich) had scrambled from Gia Lam once the navy strike package had been detected. Flying camouflaged MiG-17s, they headed towards the incoming raid at low level in an effort to avoid detection. Keeping radio silence in order to retain the element of surprise, the flight received no vectoring information from airfield controllers.

Typically, when American aircraft were detected by an observation post penetrating North Vietnamese airspace, a warning would be sent by radio or telephone. From their heading, the Vietnamese would work out which airfield they planned to hit. MiGs would then take up position in a predetermined location, staying low to avoid detection by the Americans. As the US fighter-bombers approached, the VPAF pilots would come in from behind them, increasing their speed as they closed in for the attack. Then followed a quick escape back home at low level, using their camouflage jets to blend in with the surrounding countryside.

Hanoi came under attack again on 25 April, and the MiG-17 flight of Mai Duc Toai, Le Hai, Luu Huy Chao and Hoang Van Ky claimed one F-105 over Gia Lam – the USAF credited the Thunderchief's loss to AAA. That same morning a separate raid took place on the port of Hai Phong. This time, the four MiG-17s that had been deployed to nearby Kien An the previous day remained on the ground, leaving anti-aircraft batteries to claim ten enemy aircraft destroyed. In the afternoon, a 24-aircraft 'Alpha' strike from the *Bon Homme Richard*, sailing in the Gulf of Tonkin, hit Hai Phong once again, and at 1315 hrs the MiGs at Kien An were ordered into the air.

Climbing to 1500 m over Voi mountain, the jets headed for the Van Uc river. The enemy were caught completely by surprise by the four MiG-17s, as American military intelligence believed that Kien An was still out of action. The VPAF pilots claimed three aircraft shot down, including two A-4s and one F-8. Two Skyhawks were indeed hit over the

Four g-suit-clad pilots stride out to their MiG-17Fs at Noi Bai in February 1967. The introduction of this specialist flying clothing in 1966 meant that VPAF pilots could at last make full use of the MiG's extreme manoeuvrability. The black bar immediately forward of the windscreen on the jet closest to the camera is the SRD-1M radar range-finder antenna (*Vietnamese Embassy, Budapest*)

Two flights of pilots march along the flightline at Noi Bai. Each man is wearing a white ZS-3 helmet over a leather SL-60 helmet (*Tran Dinh Kiem*)

Nguyen Van Bay, of the 923rd Fighter Regiment, pins yet another medal on his leather flying jacket. This particular award was bestowed upon him following his fifth aerial victory (an F-4), which was claimed on 24 April 1967. The VPAF's highest-scoring MiG-17 ace with seven kills, Bay was one of the pilots who flew the VPAF's first anti-ship mission on 19 April 1972 (*Tran Dinh Kiem*)

A more formal photograph of Nguyen Van Bay, showing him wearing his leather SL-60 helmet and various decorations. He flew MiG-17s with the 923rd Fighter Regiment from 1966 through to 1972 (*Tran Dinh Kiem Collection*)

target, Lt(jg) A R Crebo of VA-212 ejecting from A-4E BuNo 151102 after it had been struck by a surface-air-missile (SAM), and VA-76's Lt Charles Stackhouse being forced to abandon A-4C BuNo 147799 following a successful interception by the quartet of MiG-17 pilots. Crebo managed to nurse his damaged A-4 back out sea before ejecting, but Stackhouse failed to go 'feet wet' and was made a PoW.

The victorious MiG pilots duly disengaged and turned for home, only to discover that they had a Crusader on their tails, which chased them as far as Hai Duong. A SAM unit at Kim Thanh finally scared it off, and the relieved pilots all landed safely at Gia Lam.

In the spring of 1967 seven pilots, including MiG-17 airmen Nguyen Van Bay, Luu Huy Chao, Le Hai and Nguyen Dinh Phuc, were decorated by Ho Chi Minh for their service since the outbreak of the air war.

The ferocious aerial battles over Hanoi continued into May, with VPAF pilots flying between 30 and 40 sorties daily, and in one case as many as 78. They were proving increasingly effective, and on 12 May, three members of the 923rd claimed five kills. The flight of Cao Thanh Tinh, Le Hai, Ngo Duc Mai and Hoang Van Ky shared the credit with anti-aircraft units for the destruction of three F-4Cs over Hoa Lac – the

USAF confirmed the loss of a solitary Phantom II to MiG activity, namely F-4C 63-7614 of the 390th TFS/366th TFW, flown by Col N C Gaddis (PoW) and 1Lt J M Jefferson (MIA).

On the same day, MiG-17s with Duong Trung Tan and Nguyen Van Tho at the controls were credited with downing a F-105 over Vinh Yen, although again USAF records claim that the jet fell victim to AAA.

On 19 May Phan Thanh Tai and Nguyen Huu Diet were credited with the destruction of two navy Phantom IIs over Xuan Mai, in Hoa Binh province. However, American loss records indicate that F-4B BuNo 152264 of VF-96 (off the USS *Enterprise* (CVAN-65), and flown by Cdr R Rich (MIA) and Lt Cdr W R Stark (PoW)) and F-4B BuNo 153004 of VF-114 (from the *Kitty Hawk*, crewed by Lt(jg)s J C Plumb and G L Anderson (both PoWs)) were struck by SAMs.

With these kills, the tally of enemy aircraft on the 923rd's scoreboard reached 62 – and that same same day 'Uncle Ho' celebrated his 77th birthday. He appreciated the unit's 'present', and in return issued the regiment with a special pennant.

In May 1967 the Vietnamese claimed to have downed 85 aircraft, of which 34 were destroyed by SAMs, 32 by AAA and 19 by the VPAF – according to US sources, only two aircraft were actually lost to MiGs.

Between 24 April and 25 May, the VPAF flew 469 sorties, took part in 34 dogfights and repelled 222 American attacks.

These successes had a downside, however, for some pilots became conceited and careless, and for this they paid a heavy price. No fewer than 32 MiGs (27 of which were MiG-17s) were claimed to have been destroyed by USAF and US Navy crews in May and June alone. The loss

The 923rd's Luu Huy Chao, Le Hai, Mai Duc Toai and Hoang Van Ky were credited with shooting down an F-4B on 24 April 1967 (three were claimed by the VPAF on this day). According to American combat records one F-4B (BuNo 153000) was indeed lost, but to AAA. The fighter's crew, Lt Charles Southwick and Ens James Laing (who both became PoWs), had themselves claimed a MiG-17 (with an AIM-9B) just moments earlier. The following day, this same quartet of MiG-17 pilots downed an F-105D over Gia Lam, and again USAF loss records state that the fighter-bomber was hit by AAA. Both Luu Huy Chao and Le Hai were credited with six aerial victories apiece flying MiG-17s with the 923rd. All four pilots are seen wearing dark blue coats with a dark brown fur collar, as well as the winter-version of the SL-60 black leather helmet, and associated goggles. Note the red identification patch, marked with a yellow star and yellow 215, on Le Hai's coat (*VPAF Museum*)

On 25 April 1967, VA-76's Lt Charles D Stackhouse was shot down over Hai Phong by Nguyen Van Bay's flight whilst flying A-4C BuNo 147799. Having launched on a 24-aircraft 'Alpha' strike from the *Bon Homme Richard*, Stackhouse had dropped his bombs on the target, and was in the process of shooting a MiG-17 off his wingman's tail, when his Skyhawk was hit hard from behind. The American activated his ejection seat seconds later, and he was quickly captured. Stackhouse remained a PoW until 1973 (*VNA*)

A female member of the militia drags a section of Skyhawk wing out of the surf at Hai Phong following the 25 April 1967 clash. VA-212's Lt(jg) A R Crebo was also shot down on this mission, his A-4E (BuNo 151102) again being claimed by Nguyen Van Bay's flight. On this occasion, however, the US Navy claim that the VA-212 jet was struck by a SAM. Unlike Stackhouse, Crebo was plucked out of the sea by a navy helicopter (*Truong Van Minh*)

of so many experienced airmen in such a short space of time hurt the morale of new recruits, and by mid-1967 the total number of pilots within the two fighter regiments was less than the minimum required to staff just one of them.

There were other setbacks too. When the airfield at Kep came under attack on 19 May, the groundcrew had no time to get the MiGs off the apron, and many were damaged. The six airfields suitable for fighters – Noi Bai, Gia Lam, Hoa Lac, Kien An, Tho Xuan, as well as Kep – were repeatedly attacked, and with the exception of Noi Bai and Gia Lam, were not always quickly repaired. In the wake of these losses, Gen Van Tien Dung told the VPAF to conserve its resources, and for a time the fighters avoided action, except for a few cases, and even then only against defenceless EB-66 electronic warfare aircraft.

From the middle of June, meetings were held to discuss why the VPAF had taken such a beating in the previous weeks. It was discovered that the enemy had developed new air combat tactics, and switched to two-level formations, leaving the Vietnamese to continue its employment of now dated intercept procedures and manoeuvres. And despite ever increasing losses, some pilots still thought that random bursts of cannon fire during the course of a dogfight would ensure quick victories.

With many airmen dying in combat, those who were left now began to show signs of exhaustion through being on duty, and fighting, around the clock.

In the spring 1967, seven pilots, including Nguyen Dinh Phuc (left) and Le Hai (right), were awarded medals by Ho Chi Minh for their distinguished service throughout the air war (*via István Toperczer*)

F-4C 63-7614 of the 390th TFS/366th TFW (crewed by Col Norman Gaddis and 1Lt J M Jefferson) was downed on 12 May 1967 by Ngu Duc Mai over Hoa Luc. Local AAA units also helped secure the kill. Mai is seen here shortly after downing the Phantom II (*via István Toperczer*)

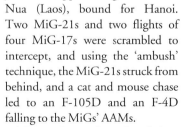

On 11 July, a MiG-17 flight successfully aided two MiG-21s of the 921st which were defending Lai Vu and Phu Luong bridges on Highway 5. Between them, they claimed an A-4 destroyed, although no losses were reported by the navy.

Ten days later the VPAF again suffered heavy losses at the hands of the Americans, when three MiG-17s were claimed to have been destroyed in a single engagement by Crusaders from VF-24 (two kills) and VF-211 (one kill). The F-8s had sortied from the *Bon Homme Richard* as fighter escorts for A-4s sent to bomb a petroleum storage facility at Ta Xa, northwest of Hai Phong.

The VPAF struck back on 23 August. At 1345 hrs radar stations reported a formation of 40 enemy aircraft approaching from Xam Nua (Laos), bound for Hanoi. Two MiG-21s and two flights of four MiG-17s were scrambled to intercept, and using the 'ambush' technique, the MiG-21s struck from behind, and a cat and mouse chase led to an F-105D and an F-4D falling to the MiGs' AAMs.

The MiG-17 pilots played their part by initiating a head-on attack. Cao Thanh Tinh and Le Van Phong then contacted their control centre by radio and continued with the air patrol. Upon discovering the F-105 strike group flying high above them,

A group of VPAF pilots from the 921st discuss tactics prior to conducting a training flight from Noi Bai in 1968. The MiG-17F 'Fresco-C' furthest from the camera has had its overall dark green paint scheme mottled with random 'splodges' of brown. Such camouflage was adopted in an effort to make the jets difficult to see both in the air and on the ground (*VPAF Museum*)

These dark green MiG-17F 'Fresco-Cs' of the 923rd Fighter Regiment are seen on the ramp at Kep. The pilots nicknamed these camouflaged aircraft 'Snakes' because of their colour scheme (*VNA*)

they initially fell behind the USAF formation, before commencing a climb in full afterburner. Once within range to fire his cannon from a position immediately astern of the last pair of F-105s, Cao Thanh Tinh opened up from 200-250 m. He closed to within 50-100 m before the leading Thunderchief went down, followed by his wingman. The second flight of MiG-17s, flown by Nguyen Van Tho and Nguyen Hong Diep, were credited with one F-4D kill.

The USAF announced the loss of two Phantom IIs from the 8th TFW's 555th TFW, with F-4D 66-0247 (flown by Capt L E Carrigan (PoW) and 1Lt C Lane (killed)) falling to the MiG-17s. No F-105s were reportedly lost, and a 34th TFS/388th TFW pilot (1Lt David Waldrop) in turn claimed a MiG-17 destroyed – all VPAF fighters returned safely to base.

Compared with the previous three months, the total number of missions flown in July, August and September was down by about two-thirds. Vietnamese fighters flew 74 missions, and were credited with nine American aircraft destroyed, whilst Waldrop's 'kill' was the only American MiG-17 claim during this period.

The enemy seemed to be concentrating once again on the destruction of North Vietnamese airfields, with Noi Bai, Kep, Hoa Lac, Kien An and Cat Bi all being attacked. Kep was hit on 24 October, although it was repaired overnight by soldiers and locals, and the following day a flight of MiG-17s from the 923rd, led by Nguyen Huu Tao, took off and claimed one F-105D destroyed. No US losses tally with this action.

With increased VPAF fighter activity came more losses for the MiG-17s, and six were claimed by US fighters during October – half of these by the 555th TFS on the 26th.

The bombing raids continued into November, with Kien An being attacked on the 17th. The runways were destroyed on this date, only to be repaired in just 48 hours by the 28th Technical Brigade.

Early on 19 November, four MiG-17s of the 923rd Fighter Regiment (piloted by Ho Van Quy, Le Hai, Nguyen Dinh Phuc and Nguyen Phi Hung) took off from Gia Lam, landing soon after at Kien An. At 1000 hrs a 20-strong 'Alpha' strike, comprised of A-4s and F-4s from the *Coral Sea*, was spotted approaching Hai Phong. The flight of MiGs immediately took off from Kien An and intercepted the enemy, Le Hai quickly downing an F-4B. A couple of minutes later two more Phantom IIs were claimed to have been shot down by Nguyen Dinh Phuc and Nguyen Phi Hung. All the MiGs returned safely to Kien An.

What follows is the American version of events on this day. VF-151's Lt(jg) James E Teague and his RIO, Lt(jg) Theodore G Stier, were flying the number two F-4B (BuNo 152304) in a two-strong flight providing cover for the strike group. As the A-4s approached the target area, the two fighters were detached to proceed north-east, where enemy aircraft were reported. The two navy fighters were tracked by radar proceeding to the assigned area, and then turning back on to a south-westerly heading as the strike group attacked. Soon after, at about 1149 hrs, while flying around the southern edge of Hai Phong, the flight leader reported MiG-17 aircraft off his right wing.

No one saw the actual engagement between the two F-4s and the MiGs. Radio transmissions were heard and recorded in which the airmen said they were engaging MiGs, that they were 'to light engine afterburners', and that they would 'break'. After a while a 'Mayday' call was heard. Other aircraft on the strike reported seeing a large fireball between 10,000-15,000 ft south-east of Cat Bi. The crew got out, although Teague died in captivity and Stier remained a PoW until March 1973. A second F-4B from VF-151 was also officially lost to VPAF fighters on this mission, BuNo 150997 being downed by Le Hai. Its crew, Lt Cdr C D Clower and Lt(jg) W O Estes also becoming PoWs.

From the middle of November air operations against Hanoi continued at a higher intensity, despite still heavier enemy losses. On 14 December an unnamed VPAF pilot reported shooting down an F-8 over Ninh Giang (not confirmed by navy records), and Crusader pilot Lt Dick Wyman, of VF-162, in turn claimed a MiG-17 destroyed during the course of this epic engagement.

Three days later a MiG-17 flight helped three MiG-21s 'bounce' a formation of 32 F-105s and F-4s heading towards the capital. While the MiG-21s scattered the bombers, and claimed down three F-105s (one was acknowledged by the USAF), the MiG-17s went in to attack the Phantom IIs, and destroyed two jets over Ha Hoa. Only F-4D 66-7774 of the 497th TFS/8th TFW was recorded as lost to VPAF fighters by US sources, its crew, Maj K R Fleenor and 1Lt T L Boyer, being captured. Forty-eight hours later a mixed formation of MiG-17s and MiG-21s claimed four kills over Tam Dao, although no losses were recorded by the Americans on this day.

In assessing the aerial encounters of 1967, the VPAF felt that their fighters were more effective while defending Hanoi and Hai Phong.

The 923rd's Nguyen Phi Hung was credited with the destruction of an F-4B over Hai Phong on 19 November 1967. However, unlike two other navy Phantom IIs (from VF-151) that were confirmed by the Americans as having been lost to MiGs, Hung's kill remained uncorroborated. He is seen here wearing the summer version of the SL-60 leather helmet over a cloth skill cap – also note his white woollen gloves (*VPAF Museum*)

Luu Huy Chao, who eventually became deputy commander of the 923rd, claimed six aerial victories between 1966 and 1968 (*Tran Dinh Kiem*)

Le Hai also scored six kills with the 923rd between 1967 and 1972. Unlike the first crop of MiG-17 pilots to serve with this regiment, Hai had received his instruction in North Vietnam with the 910th Training Regiment (*Tran Dinh Kiem*)

Co-operation between different types was good, just as it had become by that time with ADF units on the ground. A major contributing factor to the VPAF's increased effectiveness was the speedy repair of damaged airfields. Unfortunately for the pilots, the pattern seemed to be victory, defeat, reinforcement, victory, instead of a constant theme of victory, improvement, victory that was requested by their superiors.

During 1967, there were 129 instances of aerial combat, with the fighter regiments claiming 124 US aircraft destroyed – 74 of them credited to MiG-17s. American records list 24 aircraft downed in total to both MiG-17s and MiG-21s. In return, USAF crews were credited with the destruction of 41 MiG-17s, and their US Navy equivalents 12.

VISITS SOUTH

On the morning of 3 January 1968, radar units reported an EB-66C aproaching from the north-west. At 0733 hrs, American aircraft appeared over Mai Chau province, and two MiG-21s and four MiG-17s of the 923rd were scrambled from Gia Lam at 0739 hrs to effect an interception. Luu Huy Chao, Nguyen Hong Diep, Bui Van Suu and Le Hai were directed towards Thai Nguyen, but the area was blanketed with haze, preventing visual contact being made with the enemy.

Told to head for home, they suddenly spotted eight aircraft about eight kilometres away, flying on a heading of 45° to port. They turned out to be F-4Ds from the 8th TFW. The MiGs went into action. Luu Huy Chao, escorted by Nguyen Hong Diep, pushing forward on the throttle to pick up speed in an effort to harrass the Phantom IIs just as his wingman took a direct hit and was forced to eject.

Luu Huy Chao also took a pounding, but managed to keep his battered aircraft in the air and continued fighting – he was actually claimed as shot down by a crew from the 8th TFW. Veering away and down in the direction of the numerous F-4s that appeared low on his left, he accelerated and soon found himself behind the tail of a USAF jet. After firing three bursts from 700 m but seeing no hits, Luu Huy Chao disengaged, set a course for Bac Ninh and landed Noi Bai.

Meanwhile, Bui Van Suu closed on another flight of Phantom IIs, opened fire, but also missed. Turning back, he spotted yet more F-4s, and closing to within 500 m of one of them, he opened fire and apparently damaged it. Le Hai also attacked an F-4, squeezing the trigger from 800 m, but his quarry escaped unharmed. The Vietnamese pilot spent the next few minutes avoiding AAMs, and in doing so he became disorientated and ran into friendly flak over Viet Tri. Le Hai got through it and flew along the Red River to Gia Lam.

Between April and October 1968, the Americans generated 79,000 sorties against the 4th Military District from Lam River, in Nghe An province, to Gianh River, in Quang Binh. Besides defending Hanoi, the VPAF also tried to protect local transport routes, as well as fighting on front 'B' (South Vietnam) and front 'C' (Laos).

In the early spring Commander-in-Chief Nguyen Van Tien, Chief of the General Staff Tran Manh, his deputy Nguyen Phuc Trach, and high ranking officers extensively toured the 4th Military District to see what state its airfields were in, to review weather conditions and discuss enemy tactics.

They ordered the building of new airfields and the refurbishment of existing ones. Tho Xuan, in Thanh Hoa province, would soon be opened. Because of the constant repair work being carried out, the few serviceable MiGs had to regularly be sent on temporary redeployment to Noi Bai, Gia Lam, Kep, Hoa Lac, Kien An, Tho Xuan and Vinh, depending on operational requirements.

In April, the VPAF sent two MiG-17s to Vinh, but within minutes of their arrival American fighter-bombers conducted a devastating air strike on the base. The shattered remains of the two aircraft were duly stripped of useful parts, which were in turn transported back to Hanoi by truck.

A pair of MiG-17s from the 923rd was sent south again on 14 June, Luu Huy Chao and Le Hai taking off from Gia Lam at 1428 hrs and climbing to 500 m. Following the line of Highway 15 at 650 km/h, they soon reached Nghia Dan, where they continued their ascent up to 1000 m. Once over Thanh Chuong, at 1500 m, ground control warned them of six F-4s some 10° to port, at an altitude of 3000 m. The MiGs increased their speed to 730 km/h, and on reaching 2000 m Le Hai saw the enemy aircraft coasting in at right angles to them. A missile launch told them they had been spotted.

Le Hai jettisoned his external fuel tanks, accelerated to 800 km/h, evaded the oncoming missile and climbed to 2700 m. Luu Huy Chao followed his wingman and gave cover, while Le Hai turned left and tried in vain to hit one of their attackers.

The enemy leader made a steep turn, so Le Hai chose to pursue his wingman. Turning left and dropping the nose of his MiG so as to lose height, he quickly and closed on the Phantom II. He opened fire at a diatnace of 300 m, and after his second burst the F-4 caught fire and crashed into the sea (no losses were noted by the Americans on this day). Le Hai then made a left climbing turn so as to regain his original position as wingman. Suddenly, a second F-4 appeared just 1000 m in front of him, and he closed on the fighter before opening fire. However, the distance between the two jets was still too great, and he failed to hit it.

Luu Huy Chao quickly realised that the enemy were trying to get away to the south-east, so he turned to starboard and found an F-4 dead ahead. He fired, but the target was also out of range and he missed.

In an effort to provide more effective fighter cover for Hanoi and Hai Phong, the fighter regiments transferred their mobile command units to the 4th Military District in 1968 (*VPAF Museum*)

Proving the North Vietnamese peoples' total commitment to the war, children also served in the command and control centres. Here, they mark the positions of American and VPAF aircraft on a glass map (*Tran Dinh Kiem*)

Meanwhile, another Phantom II was making for the coast, and with Le Hai on his wing, Luu Huy Chao positioned himself behind his quarry and fired three bursts. The F-4 disintegrated. With the rest of the F-4s clearing the coast, the Vietnamese set course for Tho Xuan. After crossing Highway 7, they flew along Highway 15 and landed at 1500 hrs. Between 9 and 29 July, seven MiG-17s from the 923rd claimed three jets, although the Americans recorded no losses to VPAF fighters.

Mid-way through September, over Yen Thanh, Thanh Chuong and Do Luong, a mix of MiG-21s and MiG-17s were involved in an aerial engagement but failed to claim any kills. Within weeks, the Americans had increased their number of air patrols along Highways 1 and 15, and boosted radar surveillance of the region. In response, on 26 October two MiG-17s were launched to patrol over Tam Ky, where they were to lay in wait for enemy aircraft. The overcast was heavy, however, and they were unable to make visual contact and were ordered back to base. A pair of MiG-21s then tried, and 'downed' an F-4 (unconfirmed by US sources).

At the beginning of November 1968, President Johnson announced a unilateral cessation of bombing. Between 3 March 1965 and 31 October 1968, the VPAF had flown 1602 missions and claimed 218 US aircraft (of 19 different types) shot down. The Americans admitted to the loss of 50 aircraft to MiGs, and in turn claimed to have downed no fewer than 87 MiG-17s and 34 MiG-21s (plus two An-2s).

American pilots were better trained and numerically superior to their counterparts in the VPAF, although the latter had steadily improved their tactics and airmanship to the point where they could mount a satisfactory response to attacks, and provide Hanoi with effective protection.

Because of the lessons they had learned in battle, the Vietnamese were now suffering fewer losses. When the war started, North Vietnam had 36 pilots and 36 MiGs. By 1968 it had two fighter regiments with twice the number of

Pilots manning the alert flight dash to their individually camouflaged MiG-17s at Kep. The cockpit area and, in some cases, the external fuel tanks remained unpainted on VPAF 'Frescoes' (Vietnamese News Agency)

On 14 June 1968, Le Hai claimed an F-4 Phantom II destroyed near Thanh Cuong, followed just over a month later (on 19 July) by an F-8 Crusader over the 4th Military District. Neither claim tallies with known US losses, however. Note the gun camera apperture immediately above the MiG-17's gaping air intake (via István Toperczer)

pilots and five times the number of aircraft. The VPAF had become the strongest service within the PAVN.

MiG-17s IN THE 1970s

The lull in the fighting gave the North Vietnamese the chance to build up their air strength. They remained at the ready, and in 1969 pilots of the 921st and 923rd flew 540 missions.

And they still had a target to intercept in the form of the Ryan Firebee, a pilotless American reconnaissance drone, which gave them the chance for some shooting practice. Small target though it was, the 921st claimed eight of them and the 923rd two during the course of 1969.

The Firebee continued to make an appearance in 1970, when six were intercepted although none were downed. In 1971, MiGs were again scrambled six times against the type, but only one pilot was able to make a visual contact. On 9 March, Luong Duc Truong from the 923rd took off in his MiG-17 on an intercept. Spotting his prey, he closed in and shot it down. It was a costly mission, however, for Truong was killed minutes later when his jet inexplicably went out of control and crashed.

In 1971, Vietnam's military chiefs laid down the foundations for a special mission intended to deal a blow to the Americans. Ten pilots of the 923rd were picked for special ground-attack training, and with the help of Cuban advisor and pilot 'Ernesto' and his groundcrew, the Vietnamese began to train for a strike on shipping. By March 1972, six pilots were capable of flying maritime attack missions. Meanwhile, the 28th Technical Brigade was building a secret airfield at Gat, in Quang Binh province.

The 403rd radar unit was positioned near the Dinh river opposite the port of Nhat Le and given the task of keeping track of US warships.

At 1545 hrs on 18 April 1972, Le Hong Diep and Tu De of the 923rd Fighter Regiment took off from Kep. They flew their MiG-17s to Gia Lam, then on to Vinh and finally to Gat. On arrival the MiGs were quickly camouflaged and given a thorough inspection, before being handed over to the pilots selected for the mission.

Between 2300 and 2350 hrs that same day, Vietnamese radar picked up four US ships approaching the coast of Quang Binh and taking up station between ten and fifteen kilometres from the villages of Quang Xa and Ly Nhan Nam. Pilot Nguyen Van Bay clearly remembers what unfolded;

'The next day my leader, Le Xuan Di, and I were sitting in our MiG-17s preparing for the attack when, at 0930 hrs, the 403rd radar unit reported up to four ships 40 kms from Le Thuy and 120 kms from Dinh, and three ships 80 kms from the Sot river. Due to the foggy weather, we could not take off.

'At noon the radar unit reported that the ships had moved to the south, and only two remained in position. By 1500 hrs the first group of four ships was 15 kms from Ly Hoa. The second two-ship formation was seven kilometres from Quang Trach, while three more warships were 18 kms from Ly Hoa. A new group of ships was spotted at 1600 hrs 16 kms from Nhat Le.

'At 1605 hrs we received our orders to take off in the MiG-17s which had been specially converted for the bombing mission by engineer Truong Khanh Chau. We flew towards Hill 280, ten kilometres from the sea, and then turned to starboard. While flying over Ly Hoa, we saw puffs

Le Xuan Di (left) demonstrates how he and Nguyen Van Bay attacked the cruiser USS *Oklahoma City* on 19 April 1972. Di actually dropped his 250-kg bombs on the destroyer USS *Higbee*. Both ships were damaged in the surprise attack (*VPAF Museum*)

The *Gearing* class destroyer USS *Higbee* (DD-806) is seen sailing at speed in the Gulf of Tonkin just days prior to being attacked by two specially modified MiG-17Fs from the 923rd Fighter Regiment. Built during World War 2 by the Bath Ironworks, the *Higbee* was commissioned into the US Navy on 27 January 1945 and finally stricken from service on 15 July 1979 (*via István Toperczer*)

of smoke from the ships, and assumed they were firing at the coast. Le Xuan Di reported to the command that there were two ships in front of us at a distance of 10-12 kms. We received an order to attack.

'Over the sea Le Xuan Di turned to the left towards the USS *Higbee* (DD-806) and increased his speed to 800 km/h, while aiming at the ship. At a distance of 750 m he released his bombs and broke to the left. Both of the 250-kg bombs hit the ship. He reported this to ground control, and at 1618 hrs he landed at Gat airfield. His speed was too great, however, and Le Xuan Di overran the landing strip and ended up in the arrester barrier, but fortunately neither he nor his jet was damaged.

'While Le Xuan Di was attacking his target I flew on, and upon reaching the Dinh river I spotted two ships to the north-east. I was too close, and did not have time for a proper attack, so I overshot them. I had to return for a second pass, dropping my bombs from a distance of 750 m. Le Xuan Di asked me on the radio: "All right?" I answered "Not really", since I thought I had missed my target. After returning to base at 1622 hrs, I was told that a 30 m-high column of smoke was seen out at sea, and later something burst into flames.'

The attack took just 17 minutes, during which four bombs were dropped on American vessels and four seamen were wounded. *Higbee's* superstructure was badly damaged, and the rear gun structure that housed two 5-in guns completely destroyed. The flagship of the Seventh Fleet, USS *Oklahoma City* (CLG-5) sustained only minor damage.

Among the American newspapers that reported the incident on 20 April was *The Daily Independent* in Long Beach, California;

'. . . North Vietnamese MiGs, torpedo boats and shore batteries attacked US destroyers off North Vietnam on Wednesday, and the US Command reported one enemy plane was shot down and two torpedo boats were believed sunk. One MiG dropped a 250-lb (actually 250-kg) bomb on the rear deck of the Long Beach-based destroyer *Higbee*, wounding three sailors and destroying a 5-inch gun mount. Military spokesmen disclosed today that the flagship of the Seventh Fleet, the cruiser *Oklahoma City*, received minor damage from shrapnel resulting from shore fire. The American destroyers were shelling North Vietnamese coastal targets when the MiGs attacked. Torpedo boats swarming out from shore came under the guns of the guided missile frigate *Sterett* (DLG-31), the command said . . .'

In reprisal for the Vietnamese success, the Americans attacked Dong Hoi on 19 April and the airfield at Vinh the following day. A few days later US pilots discovered the airfield at Gat, and up to 30 aircraft bombed it. One MiG-17 was damaged.

On 9 May President Nixon ordered that the port of Hai Phong and other locations should be mined. At the same time, the Americans mounted deeper raids on military installations, railways and roads. The airfields at Vinh, Tho Xuan, Hoa Lac, Yen Bai and Na San were heavily bombed during the new offensive, and communication links were also badly damaged. The VPAF decided to concentrate its entire fighter force on the defence of the Hanoi and Hai Phong areas, with the MiG-17s of the 923rd Fighter Regiment operating from alongside the Hanoi-Lang Son railway line, and in the vicinity of Highway 5.

As this photograph graphically shows, the damage inflicted on the stern of the *Higbee* by Le Xuan Di's solitary 250-kg bomb was severe. It effectively wrecked the destroyer's aft 5-in turret, yet miraculously none of the vessel's crew were killed (*via István Toperczer*)

One of the largest aerial battles of 1972 took place on the morning of 10 May, when US Navy F-4s, A-6s and A-7s attacked Hai Duong and the bridges at Lai Vu and Phu Luong. Four MiG-17s from the 923rd were scrambled from Kep to protect the bridgehead at Lai Vu, and 15 kms from Hai Duong, Nguyen Van Tho and Ta Dong Trung engaged the American force. Ta Dong Trung opened fire on one of the navy jets but missed, whilst Nguyen Van Tho went after an A-7, although his aim was also poor. Realising that an F-4 was on his tail, he banked sharply and the Phantom II flew past him.

Seeing two F-4s trailing Nguyen Hang and his wingman, Nguyen Van Tho warned them of the danger, and the wingman managed to evade the Americans. Nguyen Hang was not so lucky, however, and his MiG-17 was hit by two missiles. He bailed out, but Vietnamese reports claim that he was shot dead whilst in his parachute by the two Phantom II crews that had just destroyed his aircraft – the US Navy strongly refute this claim.

Nguyen Van Tho, meanwhile, noticed that his wingman was also being chased by another F-4, and he opened fire but missed. He then ran out of ammunition. By this time Tho was also being fired on by the navy fighters, and his MiG-17 was hit by a missile. He bailed out north-west of Tu Ky. Phantom II crews from VF-96 (six kills) and VF-51 (one kill) claimed seven MiG-17s in total on the 10th.

Eight days later, four MiG-17s, along with MiG-19s and MiG-21s, tangled with hostile aircraft over Kep. The North Vietnamese were operating in pairs, supporting one another, and they managed to avoid American missiles. The American fighters started to climb and the MiG-17s followed them, and the unnamed flight leader claimed a single F-4D kill during the climbing manoeuvre at an altitude of 1500 m. The USAF recorded the loss of F-4D 66-7612, assigned to the 421st TFS/366th TFW, although no crew details are available.

Five North Vietnamese pilots of the 923rd Fighter Regiment walk down the flightline towards their 'Fresco-Cs' in 1972. The last victory for the MiG-17 was claimed on 11 July 1972, when Han Vinh Tuong shot down an F-4J over Pha Lai. According to US Navy records, no Phantom II was lost on this date, however, although F-4J BuNo 155803 from VF-103 (off the USS *Saratoga*) had been lost to a MiG 24 hours earlier (*Vietnamese Embassy, Budapest*)

After July 1972, MiG-17s from the 923rd failed to score any kills, although the unit continued to suffer losses in combat. For example, on 11 June a flight of MiGs were 'bounced' by a pair of F-4Bs from VF-51 (off the *Coral Sea*) over the Red river, and two communist jets went down – one pilot was killed. Some 17 MiG-17s were claimed by the US Navy alone in 1972-73, whilst USAF fighter crews were credited exclusively with MiG-19 and MiG-21 kills during the same period.

The final victory for Vietnam's venerable MiG-17s came on 11 July. At 0530 hrs two MiG-17s from the 923rd, flown by Han Vinh Tuong and his wingman, Hoang Cao Thang, were on a training flight over Kep when they spotted enemy fighters over Pha Lai. They were ordered to land at Noi Bai. Han Vinh Tuong immediately turned to starboard and spotted two F-4s just 5000 m away. The MiG pilots ditched their fuel tanks and attacked, and from an altitude of 1000 m and a distance of 500 m Han Vinh Tuong opened fire with his cannons. He quickly shot down one of the F-4s, and then repositioned himself to cover his wingman as they attacked another Phantom II, although this time without success.

Han Vinh Tuong failed to make it back to base, however, for he was killed when his jet was hit from behind by an AAM fired from an F-4J –

Capt Nguyen Thanh Trung (second from right) holds a briefing for MiG-17 pilots of the 923rd before leading a training flight on 25 April 1975 (*Tran Dinh Kiem Collection*)

there is no recorded US Navy MiG kill claim for this date. The navy does, however, list the loss of F-4J BuNo 155803 from VF-103 (off the USS *Saratoga* (CV-60)) on 10 July, its crew, Lts R I Randall and F J Masterson, becoming PoWs.

Proof that the MiG-17 remained very much in frontline service with the VPAF through into 1973 came in the form of the last MiG kill credited to US fighters during the Vietnam conflict. On 12 January a MiG-17 was reportedly downed with an AIM-9 by the crew of an F-4B from VF-161 off *Midway*.

Col Nguyen Nhat Chieu tells stories about the air war to schoolchildren on their visit to Bach Mai airfield, in Hanoi. A captured F-5E and an 'old' MiG-17F provide the backdrop to his speech (*VPAF Museum*)

Just 16 days later the Paris peace agreement was signed by all four warring parties, namely the US, North Vietnam, South Vietnam and the Provisional Revolutionary Government (the Viet Cong). The American air strikes immediately stopped, allowing the remnants of the VPAF's fighter force to commence re-equipment, and the various bases around Hanoi and Hai Phong to be repaired. Within days of the ceasefire being announced, the 923rd relocated its MiG-17s to Tho Xuan, where it kept two fully-armed jets on constant alert. Just a handful of fighters were left at Kien An to defend Hai Phong, and the final training of much-needed replacement MiG-17 pilots got underway in earnest within the 923rd at Kien An, Tho Xuan, Vinh and Dong Hoi.

The venerable MiG-17 remained in frontline service with the VPAF until the late 1970s, the 923rd re-rolling in the ground attack and maritime strike missions, leaving fighter interception to those regiments equipped with MiG-21s. Eventually employed as a lead-in fighter trainer, the last examples of the MiG-17 were finally retired in the early 1980s.

Several years after the cessation of hostilities, a new generation of VPAF fast jet pilots listen to Pham Tuan as he tells them about his experiences dogfighting the Americans (*Truong Van Minh*)

'FARMERS' OF THE SKY

In February 1969 North Vietnam was enjoying a four-month break from American air raids. In an effort to boost the VPAF's fighter strength, defence chiefs decided to create the 925th Fighter Regiment (Trung Doan Khong Quan Tiem Kich 925) and equip it with MiG-17Fs and Shenyang J-6s (Chinese-built MiG-19s). Nguyen Quang Trung was appointed as the regiment's CO, and the unit was established at Yen Bai. This facility had just one runway, with electricity provided by generators.

The unit's preparation for battle was hampered by fuel shortages and a high hardware attrition rate caused by humid climate, poor maintenance and inadequate logistical support. Pilots of the 925th came from Gia Lam, having first passed through Soviet flying schools, where they had been trained on the MiG-21. At Yen Bai, intense training produced nine combat-rated MiG-19 pilots by April 1969.

GREAT BATTLES OF MAY

By the spring of 1972, the MiG-19 pilots had matured into an effective element within the air defence system. And this was just as well, for compared with the Johnson administration's bombing campaigns of 1965-68, President Nixon's series of offensives were bigger affairs altogether. For example, as part Operation *Freedom Train* on 6 April

The first 44 Chinese-built J-6s (MiG-19S 'Farmer-Cs') arrived with the 925th Fighter Regiment in 1968-69. In this undoubtedly posed photograph, the unit's commander demonstrates dogfighting manoeuvres to his pilots at Yen Bai with the aid of two scale models of the MiG-19. All are wearing old style leather helmets and plain flight suits, both of which were soon discarded in favour of more modern 'bone domes' and g-suits. Photographs of the MiG-19 in VPAF service are rare, reflecting the small number of 'Farmers' supplied to the air force (*VPAF Museum*)

North Vietnamese pilots rush to their J-6s in early 1972 at Yen Bai during a practice scramble. Had this been for real, the aircraft behind them would have been surrounded by ground personnel preparing the jets for take-off. An AAM launch rail can just be made out on the wing of the second 'Farmer' in this line-up (*Tran Dinh Kiem Collection*)

1972, US pilots flew no less than 106 raids on Quang Binh province alone. Four days later B-52s attacked Vinh. On 13 April they turned their attention to Thanh Hoa, and three days later B-52s and naval units pounded Hai Phong.

VPAF commanders decided that its forces should take up position to the north of the 20th Parallel, and the 925th Fighter Regiment was duly tasked with defending North Vietnam's western and north-western airspace. Under Operation *Pocket Money*, at the beginning of May, Nixon announced the mining of the North's most important ports.

On the 8th of that month, when Operation *Linebacker* was launched, the 925th was told to mount a constant CAP over Yen Bai air base to protect the Thac Ba hydroelectric power station – the 921st was to help by distracting the Americans. The plan involved the 925th having two flights of MiGs at opposite ends of Yen Bai. No 1 flight, towards the north, consisted of four MiG-19s flown by Nguyen Ngoc Tiep, Nguyen Duc Tiem, Pham Hung Son and Nguyen Hong Son. No 2 flight patrolled further to the south, and was comprised of Nguyen Ngoc Tam, Nguyen Thanh Long, Phung Van Quang and Nguyen Manh Tung.

The morning of the 8th saw radar units detect four aircraft 35 kms south-west of Moc Chau, heading for Yen Bai at an altitude of 5000 m. Two MiG-21s from the 921st took off at 0840 hrs and headed towards Tuyen Quang. Seven minutes later No 1 flight also took to the air.

The quartet of MiG-19s broke through cloud cover at between 1000-1200 m, and turned to port. By 0852 hrs they were at 4000 m. Pham Hung Son then spotted the Americans at 40° to his right, some six kilometres away, and at an altitude of 4000 m. He reported this to the MiG-21 flight.

Veteran fighter controller Nguyen Van Chuyen (centre, speaking into the microphone) follows the progress of US aircraft on radar, and in turn directs MiG-19s against them (*via István Toperczer*)

Three pilots serving with the 925th Fighter Regiment became well known for their similar names – Nguyen Hong Son, Pham Hung Son and Nguyen Hung Son, who were quickly dubbed 'Son A', 'Son B' and 'Son C', respectively. All three were successful in downing enemy aircraft, and they became the best-known MiG-19 airmen of the war. Nguyen Hong Son (A), seen in this photograph, claimed an F-4 destroyed over Yen Bai on 8 May 1972, although American records fail to note any losses to VPAF activity on this date. Two days later his MiG was struck by an AAM, and although he successfully ejected from his stricken fighter, 'Son A' was fatally injured on landing. Although US Phantom II crews were credited with the destruction of seven MiG-17s and four MiG-21s on 10 May, no one claimed a MiG-19 kill. Perhaps one of the MiG-17s was incorrectly identified during the confusion of battle, or was 'Son A' struck by an ADF SAM? (*VPAF Museum*)

Nguyen Ngoc Tiep also radioed that he had spotted four F-4s. The American crews then saw that they had company, and launched a series of AAMs which all missed. Nguyen Ngoc Tiep ordered everyone to attack. The Phantom IIs split into pairs, and Nguyen Ngoc Tiep and Nguyen Duc Tiem went after the jets that broke to the left and Pham Hung Son and Nguyen Hong Son chased the pair that went right.

As Nguyen Duc Tiem pursued the F-4s, he noticed that missiles were coming at him from another Phantom II – hard manoeuvring got him out of trouble. Nguyen Ngoc Tiep stuck to his F-4 as it dived to 1500 m and tried to escape with a left turn. He increased his speed and opened up with his cannons, only to miss as the target flew into cloud.

Nguyen Ngoc Tiep then turned to the right, and something else took his attention – two F-4s at 2000 m. One tried to get into cloud but the Vietnamese pilot fired his cannon and reported scoring numerous hits. Tiep stated that the F-4 went down, but USAF records do not corroborate his claim.

Another Phantom II chased by Pham Hung Son and Nguyen Hong Son descended quickly to 1500 m, and the lead MiG pilot fired at it in vain. The American pilot then climbed to 2000 m, followed by Son, and the pair vanished into cloud.

During the confusion of battle, Nguyen Hong Son tried to drop his fuel tanks but pulled the wrong lever. The brake chute deployed instead, and it was instantly ripped away. At the same time Nguyen Ngoc Tiep thought he saw an American pilot ejecting.

Eventually Nguyen Hong Son managed to get rid of his fuel tanks, only to see he was being lined up by an AAM. He only escaped thanks to a sudden dive.

His attacker followed him, but because of his greater speed he overran the MiG-19, and it was Nguyen Hong Son who now became the hunter. The Phantom II flew into a cloud, but Nguyen Hong Son pressed on, and when they had closed to within 500 m of each other he fired again. Son noticed flames streaming from the back of the Phantom II, but broke off his attack when he spotted a mountain looming large in front of him. He made it safely back to Yen Bai.

Nguyen Ngoc Tiep was now down to his last 1100 litres of fuel, but he remained on station until two MiG-19s arrived to take over from him. By 0916 hrs all the 'Farmers' were safely back at base.

The Vietnamese constantly analysed their enemy's tactics with the help of information provided by their own pilots or gleaned through interrogation of captured American airmen. The VPAF had soon realised that US fighters avoided turning with the agile MiG-17s and MiG-19s, and instead placed great emphasis on quickly gaining or losing height. Their aircraft entered combat with the leader and wingman well spaced, as this formation required less concentration to maintain position, and allowed pilots to pay more attention on visually spotting MiGs trying to sneak up on them. When facing a lone MiG, US crews would work together to ensure a kill, and when meeting a pair of MiGs, they would invariably go after the wingman. If encountering a larger formation, they would separate and engage individual MiGs in pairs.

Besides mining the waters of Hai Phong and other ports, the Americans also targeted the airfields of Vinh, Tho Xuan, Hoa Lac, Yen Bai and Na San during the month of May. On the 9th, 200 aircraft were launched against these bases, as well as the major roads around Hanoi and Hai Phong. These attacks were anticipated, and the strength of the four fighter regiments was concentrated on trying to beat them off.

On 10 May US raiders hit Hai Phong, Bac Ninh, Pha Lai, Son Dong and Luc Ngan. While some jets attacked north of Hanoi, others kept a close watch on the bases at Noi Bai, Hoa Lac and Kep. Two MiG-21s of the 921st scrambled from Noi Bai at 0944 hrs and headed for Tuyen Quang in an effort to distract the attention of patrolling American fighters away from the MiG-19s of the 925th's No 1 flight.

Despite this ruse, 'Farmer' pilots Nguyen Ngoc Tiep and Nguyen Duc Tiem found themselves in action within seconds of taking off, chasing enemy aircraft and firing their cannons, but failing to make any

VPAF MiG-19 crews met the enemy for the first time in early May 1972, and during this month they claimed seven US aircraft destroyed (all were identified as F-4 Phantom IIs). Only two of these victories can be corroborated by American records, however. USAF Phantom II crews claimed three MiG-19 kills during the same period, and two 'Farmers' were also credited to the US Navy's VF-161, flying F-4Bs from the *Midway* (*via István Toperczer*)

Pilots and the commander of Flights 1 and 2 discuss the battles of 8 and 10 May at Yen Bai. Although still wearing leather helmets, they have all been issued with green nylon PPK-1 anti-g trousers (*VPAF Museum*)

impression on their enemies. Fifteen minutes later, squadron-mate Pham Hung Son enjoyed much greater success when fired his cannons at an F-4E some 2000 m in front of him. The Phantom II was hit hard, and Son pressed home his attack, firing again from 300 m. F-4E 67-0386 of the 58th TFS/432nd TRW broke in two, killing its crew, Capts J L Harris (pilot) and D E Wilkinson (WSO). Moments later Son's wingman, Nguyen Hong Son, was hit by a missile (possibly a SAM) over La Mount, in Tuyen Quang province. He ejected, but later died of his injuries.

No US claims against MiG-19s were made on this day, although Maj Barton P Crews and Capt Keith W Jones (flying F-4D 66-7463) of the 13th TFS/432nd TRW had been awarded a MiG-19 kill 48 hours earlier – conversely, no VPAF losses were recorded on the 8th!

The encounter on 10 May had lasted just 20 minutes, yet the MiG pilots were already running low on fuel. No 2 flight was duly scrambled so that it pilots could provide cover while No 1 landed. Nguyen Duc Tiem had completely run out of fuel by the time he touched down, and having approached too fast from a height of 1600 m, he overshot. His MiG was badly damaged, but he was safe.

Nguyen Ngoc Tiep and Pham Hung Son were also on their approach, landing gear extended, when more F-4s appeared. Pham Hung Son

Pham Hung Son ('Son B') made his first contact with the enemy on 8 May 1972, attempting unsuccessfully to down a Phantom II with cannon fire. His fortunes changed dramatically two days later, however, for he destroyed F-4E 67-0386 of the 58th TFS/432nd TRW, killing its crew, Capts J L Harris (pilot) and D E Wilkinson (WSO). On 23 May he was credited with the destruction of a second Phantom II, which was duly commemorated by the North Vietnamese as the 3600th enemy aircraft shot down over the north. According to American records, no combat aircraft were lost to VPAF activity on this day (*VPAF Museum*)

retracted his undercarriage and covered his leader while the latter pilot landed, before he, too, had a chance to get back down.

No 2 flight had also found itself in a scrap moments after take-off, Nguyen Manh Tung firing twice at F-4D 65-0784 of the 555th TFS/432nd TRW. This particular machine was being flown by Maj Robert Lodge and Capt Roger Locher, who, minutes earlier, had claimed a MiG-21 kill – this was their third victory (all scored in 65-0784) since February. The tables were turned on this occasion, however, for the Phantom II was literally blown out of the sky. Only Capt Locher survived, the WSO being recovered by a Combat SAR helicopter.

Phung Van Quang also attacked another F-4, firing three times, but he failed to score any hits. No 2 flight's encounter took place over an 18-minute period, and even though US fighters were still in the immediate area, the MiG pilots were told to land due to their rapidly dwindling reserves of fuel.

Nguyen Ngoc Tam touched down safely, but Phung Van Quang overran by 50 m without harming himself, or damaging his aeroplane. Nguyen Manh Tung left his landing too late, however, running out of fuel on his approach. Having descended from a height of 1400 m, he came down too fast and over-ran the end of the runway. Tung's MiG turned over and exploded, killing him instantly.

Only Nguyen Thanh Long was now still airborne, and just as he was about to land a warning crackled over his radio telling him that there were F-4s on his tail. He turned away, and luckily for him so did the Americans, who headed home.

By 1047 hrs the fight was over. The eight North Vietnamese pilots from the 925th had fired off 1050 rounds of 30 mm ammunition, and had claimed two USAF Phantom IIs. Only one MiG-19 had been shot down, although two pilots and two aircraft had been lost.

In the second half of May 1972, encounters with the Americans became increasingly fierce, and with enemy aircraft reguarly attacking Yen Bai, elements of the 925th had to be relocated to Gia Lam.

The war diary of the regiment during this frenetic period was filled with some victories, but also many losses. For example, on 12 May four MiG-19s again clashed with a flight of F-4Ds from the 555th TFS/432nd TRW, and a solitary MiG-19 went down.

During this stage of the conflict, VPAF pilots were usually outnumbered when they engaged the enemy, and this was very much the case on 18 May. In the morning, four MiG-19s had downed F-4D 66-7612 of the 421st TFS/366th TFW (names and fate of the crew unknown) over Noi Bai, but that afternoon, two MiGs had attacked a formation of twelve *Midway*-based F-4Bs over Kep. Both jets had been quickly despatched by Sidewinders fired from two VF-161 Phantom IIs, killing the Vietnamese pilots. And on 23 May, four MiG-19s of No 1 flight took on 16 F-4Es from the 35th TFS/366th TFW over Yen Bai. Pham Hung Son and Nguyen Hung Son each claimed one kill (no USAF losses were recorded), while Nguyen Duc Tiem fell to friendly fire in the shape of a SAM fired by the ADF. The pilot managed to eject. The 35th TFS credited one of its crews with a single MiG-19 kill on this day.

Vietnamese SAMs claimed yet another VPAF MiG-19 on 2 June, and this time the pilot was not so lucky. Four jets had been scrambled from Gia

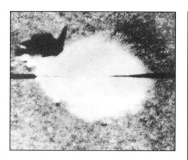

This still from Pham Hung Son's gun camera film was reportedly taken on 23 May 1972, and it shows a USAF Phantom II after it had been hit by cannon fire. The fireball that has erupted behind the seemingly stricken jet is clearly visible (*via István Toperczer*)

Nguyen Hung Son ('Son C') is seen here in a classic fighter pilot's pose, standing in the cockpit of his MiG-19. Little detail regarding his exploits have so far come to light, other than the fact that the destruction of the 3601st American aircraft over North Vietnam was attributed to him on 23 May 1972. This was the seventh, and last, victory credited to the MiG-19 in VPAF service, 'Son C's' F-4 being downed over Yen Bai (*VPAF Museum*)

Lam after F-4s were spotted over Kep. In the ensuing engagement, the battling fighters drifted over Bac Giang, and the flight leader's MiG-19 was hit, was killing him instantly. The USAF credited the demise of this 'Farmer' to Maj Philip Handley and 1Lt John Smallwood of the 58th TFS/432nd TRW, flying F-4E 67-210 – the crew claimed it as a guns kill

Both 'friendly' fire losses were caused by a lack of communication between ADF anti-aircraft batteries on the ground and the VPAF fighters overhead. Vietnamese ground units had been using old Chinese-made radar fitted with the 'Kremnij 1' system, whilst the MiG-19s and SAM units relied on more modern, Russian-made, 'Kremnij 2' equipment. The interface between the two systems proved to be very poor in the heat of battle, resulting in the demise of two MiG-19s and the death of a highly-trained fast jet pilot.

In July and August, the 925th failed to score any further kills, but conversely did not lose any pilots in combat. In September and October, however, two American aircraft were reportedly downed in three encounters, although no details pertaining to these claims have emerged. The VPAF has admitted the loss of a further three MiG-19s during these engagements, and the the USAF credited its crews with four kills – on 2 September, 9 September (two kills) and 6 October. All four calims were by F-4D/E crews.

With only a handful of the 54 MiG-19Ss (actually Chinese-built Shenyang J-6s) supplied in 1968-69 still operational by the autumn of 1972, VPAF 'Farmer' operations quietly fizzled out.

Kien An subsequently became the HQ for both the 921st and 925th Fighter Regiments, the latter being re-equipped with 24 Chinese-built MiG-19s (F-6s) in 1974. Following the arrival of these machines, the regiment manned a two aircraft alert flight at Yen Bai tasked with defending north-western Hanoi.

By May 1975 it was clear that military action was coming to an end in the region, even along the frontline in South Vietnam. Flying activity was reduced accordingly, and the MiG-19s were now equipped only with training weaponry. The reduction in flying did not prevent accidents from occurring, however. For example, while preparing for an air display to celebrate the North Vietnamese victory in 1975, two MiG-19s collided in mid-air over Noi Bai. After the tragedy, the runway was cleared of the wrecked aircraft and flying resumed – just as if nothing had happened!

North Vietnamese Prime Minister Pham Van Dong (right) talks with MiG-19 pilots of the 925th Fighter Regiment at Yen Bai just days after the epic clashes in May 1972 (*via István Toperczer*)

On 25 December 1975, the 370th 'Hai Van' Air Division (Su Doan Khong Quan 370) was established, incorporating the 925th Fighter Regiment, the MiG-19s of the 371st Air Division, a flight of ex-South Vietnamese air force Cessna U-17 Skywagons and South Vietnamese air control units.

The 370th continued to fly a handful of surviving 'Farmers' as lead-in fighter trainers until the end of the 1970s.

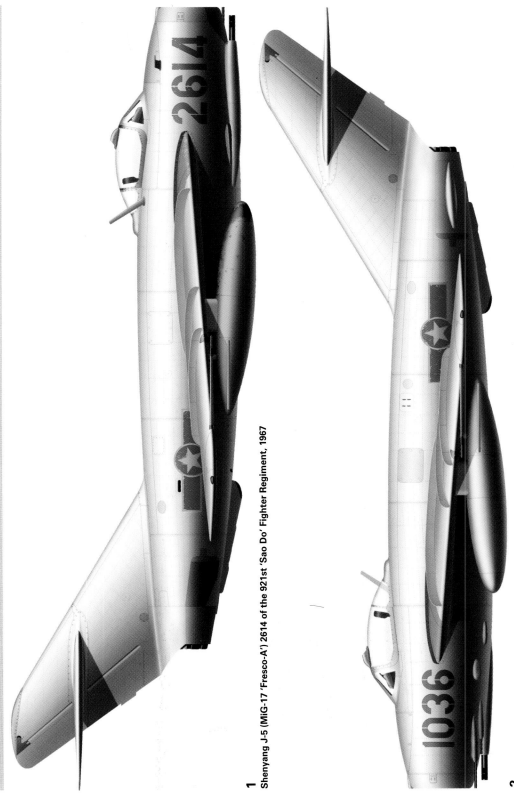

1
Shenyang J-5 (MiG-17 'Fresco-A') 2614 of the 921st 'Sao Do' Fighter Regiment, 1967

2
Shenyang J-5 (MiG-17 'Fresco-A') 1036 of Le Minh Huan, 921st 'Sao Do' Fighter Regiment, 4 April 1965

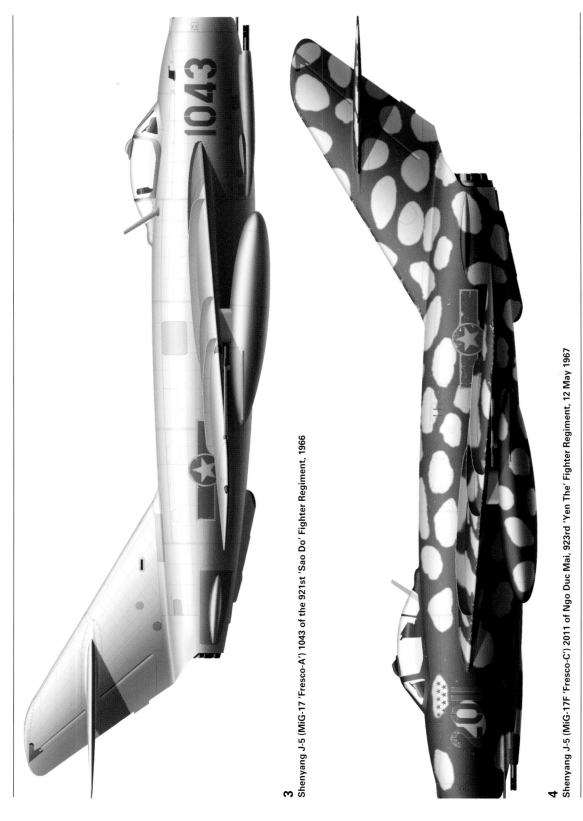

3
Shenyang J-5 (MiG-17 'Fresco-A') 1043 of the 921st 'Sao Do' Fighter Regiment, 1966

4
Shenyang J-5 (MiG-17F 'Fresco-C') 2011 of Ngo Duc Mai, 923rd 'Yen The' Fighter Regiment, 12 May 1967

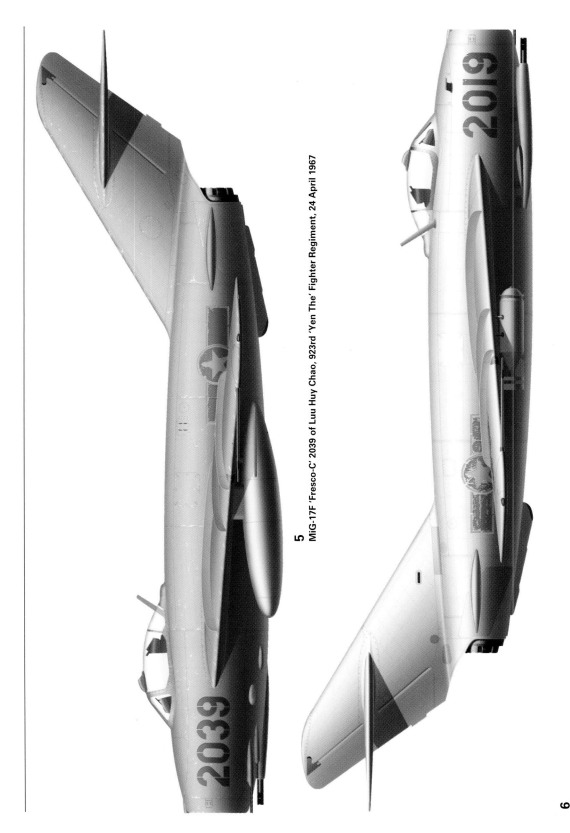

5
MiG-17F 'Fresco-C' 2039 of Luu Huy Chao, 923rd 'Yen The' Fighter Regiment, 24 April 1967

6
MiG-17F 'Fresco-C' 2019 of Le Xuan Di, 923rd 'Yen The' Fighter Regiment, 19 April 1972

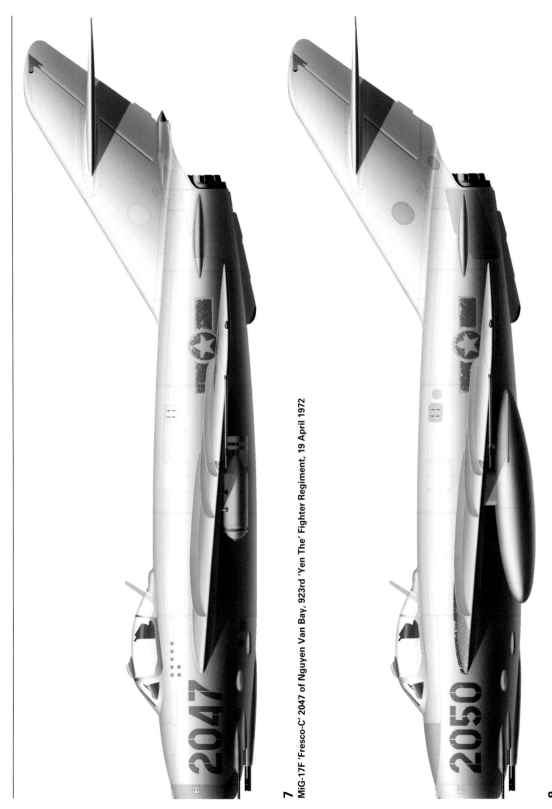

7
MiG-17F 'Fresco-C' 2047 of Nguyen Van Bay, 923rd 'Yen The' Fighter Regiment, 19 April 1972

8
Shenyang J-5 (MiG-17F 'Fresco-C') 2050 of Pham Ngoc Lan, 921st 'Sao Do' Fighter Regiment, 6 November 1965

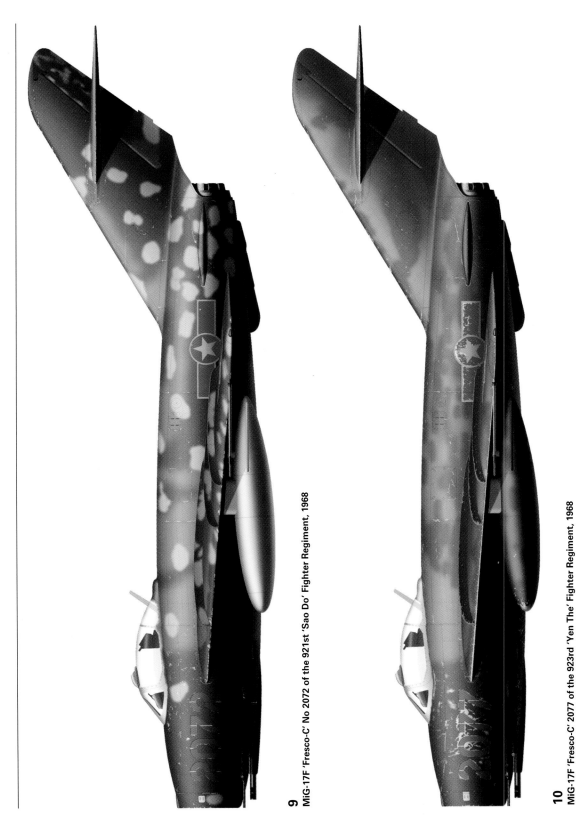

9
MiG-17F 'Fresco-C' No 2072 of the 921st 'Sao Do' Fighter Regiment, 1968

10
MiG-17F 'Fresco-C' 2077 of the 923rd 'Yen The' Fighter Regiment, 1968

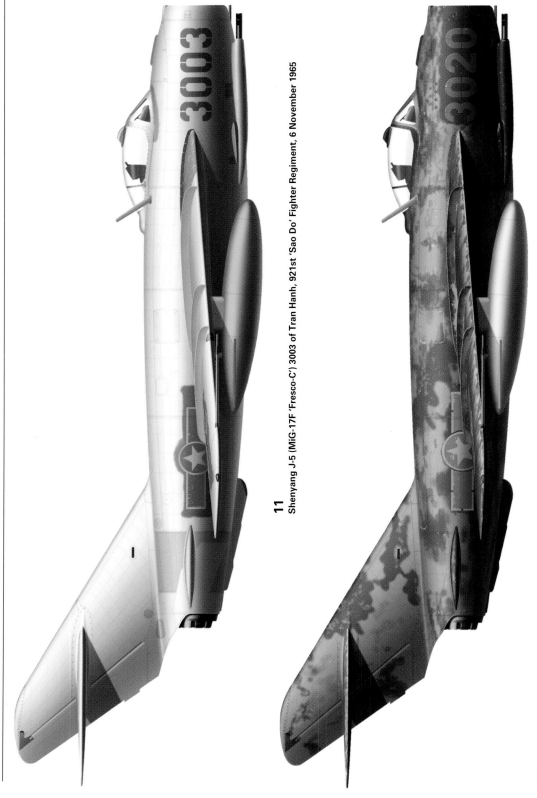

11
Shenyang J-5 (MiG-17F 'Fresco-C') 3003 of Tran Hanh, 921st 'Sao Do' Fighter Regiment, 6 November 1965

12
MiG-17F 'Fresco-C' 3020 of Le Hai, 923rd 'Yen The' Fighter Regiment, 14 June 1968

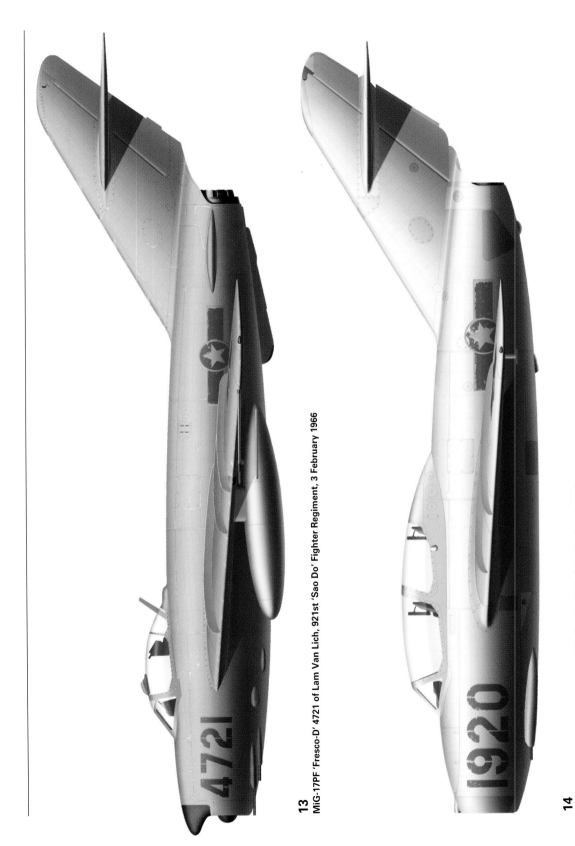

13
MiG-17PF 'Fresco-D' 4721 of Lam Van Lich, 921st 'Sao Do' Fighter Regiment, 3 February 1966

14
MiG-15UTI 'Midget' 1920 of the 910th 'Julius Fucik' Training Regiment, 1965

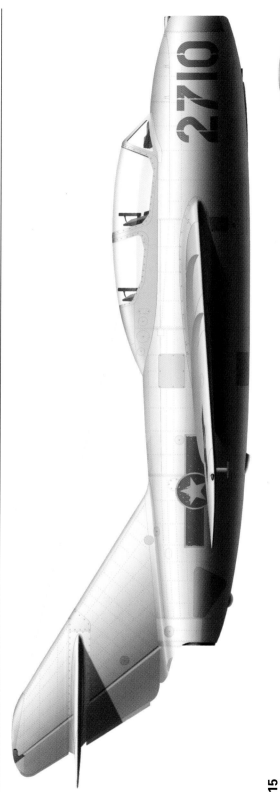

15
MiG-15UTI 'Midget' 2710 of the 910th 'Julius Fucik' Training Regiment, 1964

16
Shenyang JJ-5 1505 of the 910th 'Julius Fucik' Training Regiment, 1967

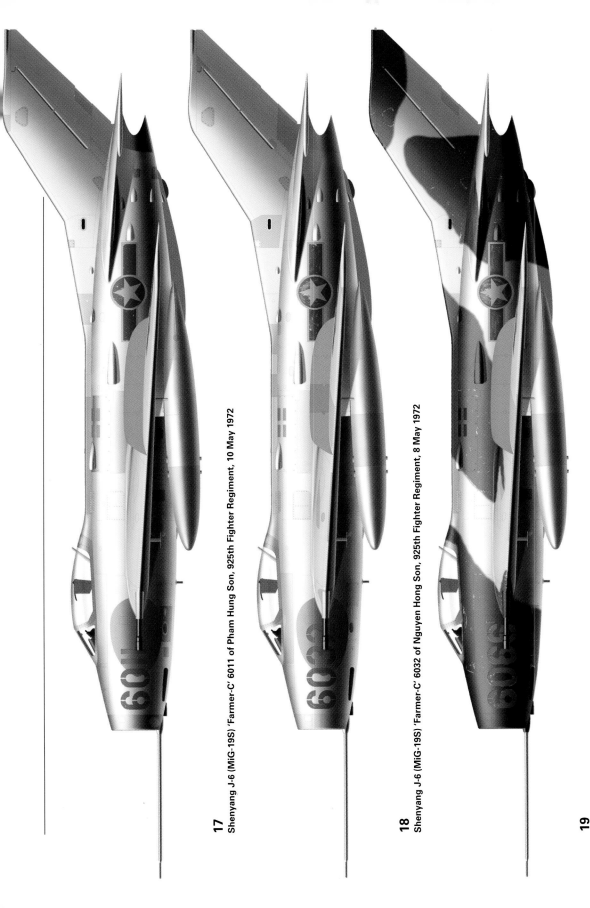

17
Shenyang J-6 (MiG-19S) 'Farmer-C' 6011 of Pham Hung Son, 925th Fighter Regiment, 10 May 1972

18
Shenyang J-6 (MiG-19S) 'Farmer-C' 6032 of Nguyen Hong Son, 925th Fighter Regiment, 8 May 1972

19
Shenyang J-6 (MiG-19S) 'Farmer-C' 6066 of the 925th Fighter Regiment, 1972

1

2

3

4

5

6

7

8

9

10

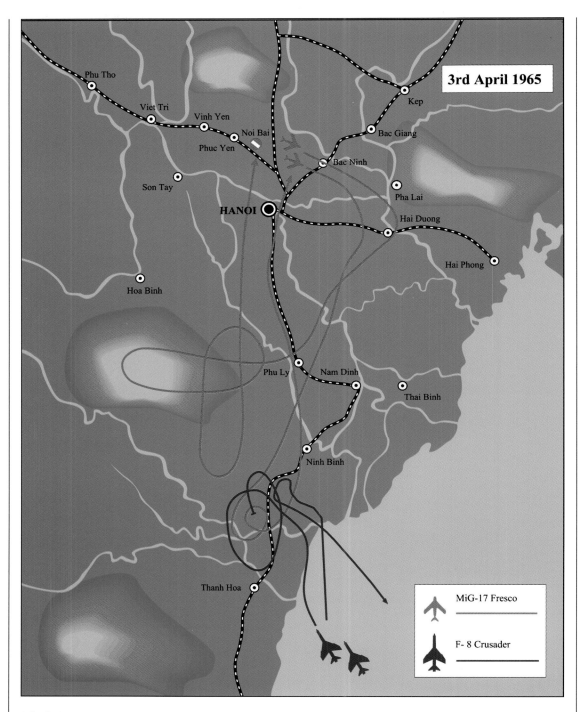

3rd April 1965

MiG-17 Fresco

F- 8 Crusader

3 April 1965
Pham Ngoc Lan and Phan Van Tuc attack two F-8 Crusaders of VF-211 over Thanh Hoa province

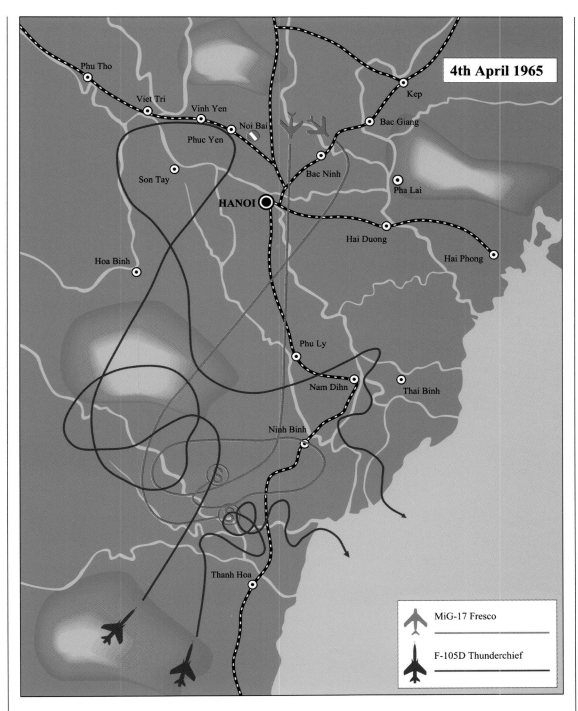

MiG-17 Fresco

F-105D Thunderchief

4 April 1965
Tran Hanh and Le Minh Huan shoot down two F-105Ds (59-1754 and 59-1764, both from the 355th TFW) over Ham Rong

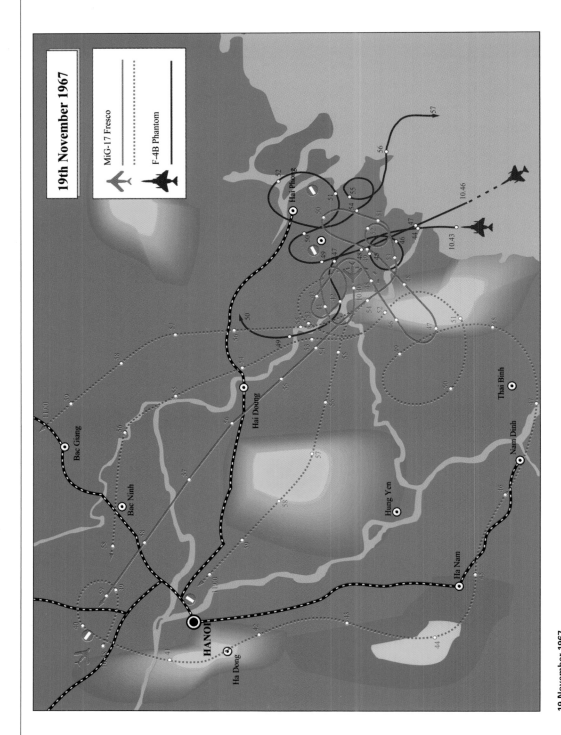

19 November 1967
Two F-4Bs (BuNos 150997 and152304, both from VF-151) off the USS *Coral Sea* are shot down over Hai Phong by Le Hai and Nguyen Dinh Phuc

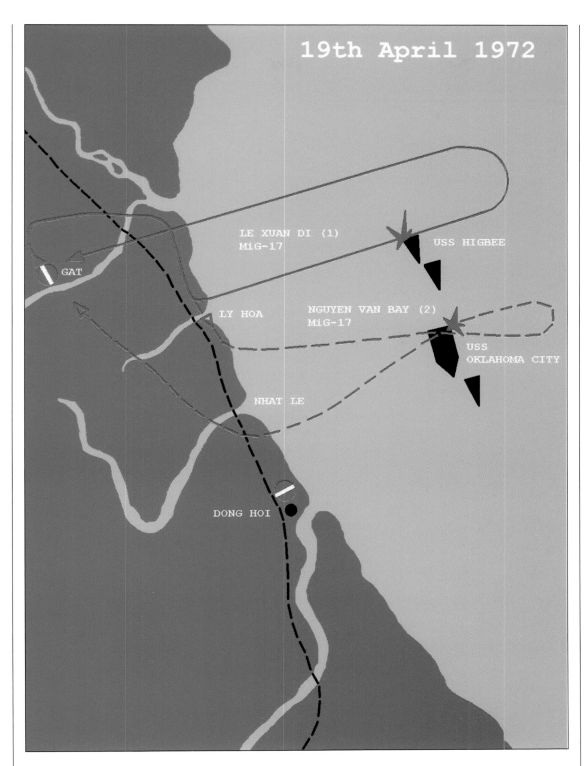

LE XUAN DI (1)
MiG-17

USS HIGBEE

GAT

LY HOA

NGUYEN VAN BAY (2)
MiG-17

USS
OKLAHOMA CITY

NHAT LE

DONG HOI

19 April 1972
Two modified MiG-17F fighter-bombers (flown by Nguyen Van Bay and Le Xuan Di) of the 923rd Fighter Regiment attack the USS *Higbee* and USS *Oklahoma City* in the Gulf of Tonkin

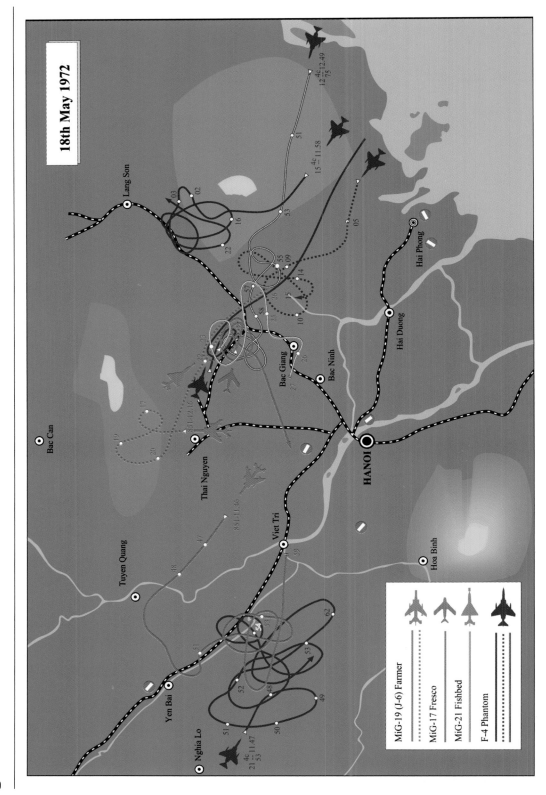

18th May 1972

MiG-19 (J-6) Farmer

MiG-17 Fresco

MiG-21 Fishbed

F-4 Phantom

18 May 1972
Two Phantom IIs are attacked, and claimed to have been destroyed, by MiG-17, MiG-19 and MiG-21 fighters (only F-4D 66-7612 of the 366th TFW was confirmed destroyed)

CORKSCREW AND HAMMER

North Vietnam had always been a grateful recipient of military aid from China, the Soviet Union and other communist countries such as Czechoslovakia, East Germany, Hungary and Poland. However, it had tried hard to become self-reliant when it came to maintaining the weaponry that these countries had supplied.

The air force had trained its first technical personnel on courses organised by the Air Force Research Committee as early as 1949. In March 1956, the Airfield Research Committee started training technical officers whose job it would be to set up the support infrastructure (such as maintenance workshops) crucial for the day-to-day running of any air force. And from 1957 onwards, technicians as well as pilots were sent abroad to further hone their skills. By 1960, some 200 students had graduated from technical schools in the Soviet Union and China.

Things really started to happen at home when defence chiefs set up the A-33 Aircraft Repair Facility (Xuong Sua Chua May Bay A-33) at Bach Mai, in Hanoi, on 10 April 1961. Assisted by foreign specialists, the VPAF also established maintenance training courses, and by 1965 the facility had dedicated sections for the repair of helicopters and MiG-17s.

At the end of that year, MiG-21F-13 and MiG-17PFs started arriving from the Soviet Union, and these were rapidly assembled with the help of Russian advisers. Initially it took up to ten days to put each aircraft together at the A-33, but with continually improving technical skills, the time taken was reduced to a week and, finally, just three days. Aside from assembling new fighters, technicians also had an increasing number of aircraft to maintain as well – three times more than in the early war years.

With the escalation of the conflict, the workload of the technical units increased massively, and particularly so between 1965 and 1968. As well as having to deal with battle damage, groundcrews also had to cope with the humid air of South-East Asia, which played havoc with the avionics fitted in the MiGs.

Although combat and climate posed problems for the VPAF, the greatest difficulty facing the Vietnamese was an insufficient reserve of mechanical engineers. More frequent training programmes

Like virtually all major VPAF airfields, Kep was attacked on a near daily basis during the major US bombing offensives. And like those other bases, it was usually back in action the day after an air strike thanks to the help of literally thousands of local residents, who would work ceaselessly until the runways were declared operational once again. Here, the return of a camouflaged MiG-17F from a patrol has provoked no response from local farmers busy filling in bomb craters (*via István Toperczer*)

The photographs on this page show battle-damaged MiG-17F 'Fresco-Cs' of the 923rd Fighter Regiment undergoing maintenance in makeshift bamboo hangars. Such facilities provided good camouflage against American bombers, for the huts were usually located in villages or agricultural co-operatives, making them difficult to spot from the air. Seeing these field maintenance conditions, one can easily understand why the VPAF suffered such a high attrition rate with its jet fighters (*VPAF Museum*)

helped ease the situation a little, but the air force struggled in this area for the duration of the conflict.

Despite the shortage of qualified groundcrew, A-33 engineers Truong Khanh Chau and Huynh Ngoc An, backed by a group of technicians, rebuilt 11 aircraft, repaired damage to eight others, changed the engines in 12 and assembled 24 brand new fighters in 1968 alone. Modification work was also carried out, including the changing of the hydraulic dampeners on the entire MiG-17 force.

At the beginning of 1969, the maintenance crews on each aircraft were each short of one mechanic, and in some cases even two. Overall, there

Technicians install an external store of unknown purpose on the outer port wing hardpoint of a MiG-17. The lens suggests some kind of optical device – perhaps a reconnaissance camera. The aircraft is parked inside a concrete shelter built within a mountain cavern, which provided undisturbed working conditions. The MiG-17 would have been deposited at this remote site by a Mil-6, and then pushed inside by a truck (*VPAF Museum*)

were just 43 qualified personnel available to service the entire VPAF MiG-17 force, instead of the 120 that were needed. With the increase in aircraft numbers, the long term effects of the weather and the inevitable lack of proper maintenance during heightened periods of operational activity, most 'Frescoes' were in a poor state of disrepair by the spring of 1968. A vast amount of work would be need to be expended to keep them airworthy.

The VPAF also had 774 trucks, but that was only about 70 per cent of the number it needed to function properly. They were maintained by 476 drivers, all of whom had to fight to secure spare parts, and working space in which to fix their vehicles. Consequently, the vehicles would frequently break down, creating constant problems when it came to ensuring that the VPAF had sufficient fuel with which to fly its MiGs.

To make matters worse, 40 different types of fuel had been scattered among 500 tanks in 48 different locations in an effort to make it harder for

A MiG-17 tail section is inspected from the inside by an engineer from the A-33 Aircraft Repair Facility (*VPAF Museum*)

North Vietnamese groundcrews prepare a quartet of MiG-17s for their next mission at Noi Bai. Note the two technicians manhandling the engine starter cart across the apron to a waiting fighter out of shot (*VNA*)

Mil's hugely impressive Mi-6 could easily lift fully-armed and refuelled MiG-17s, and transport them from their dispersals in the mountains to jet-capable airfields. After completing their missions, the fighters would soon be delivered back and hidden from enemy fighter-bombers. The VPAF's modest fleet of Mil-6s transported MiG-17s on approximately 400 occasions to remote mountain shelters up to 30 kms away from operational bases (*VPAF Museum*)

the Americans to target dumps. This was a sound plan when the air force's fleet of trucks was fully serviceable, but it became a logistical nightmare when technical maladies gripped the transport arm of the VPAF. Shortages of other supplies also had a grave impact on the effectiveness of other specialists, such as telegraphists and wireless operators.

In 1970, pressure on maintenance crews eased somewhat when the decision was made to send damaged aircraft abroad for overhaul. Upon their return, they were dispersed to newly-built earth shelters at the airfields at Kien An, Hoa Lac, Ha Bac and Lang Son. Interim maintenance was carried out at Yen Bai, Noi Bai and Kep. On more than 400 occasions fighters were slung beneath massive Mil Mi-6 helicopters for swift movement to maintenance facilities or dispersal areas.

THE MASTER

Just as the exploits of the leading MiG aces such as Nguyen Van Bay and Luu Huy Chao made them legends amongst the flying fraternity of the VPAF, for groundcrews, the master of their trade was Truong Khanh Chau. He had enrolled in the fledgling VPAF in the early 1950s, and over the years had introduced several innovative ideas and modifications for different single-role aircraft that had made them suitable for a variety of

Right
The entire aft section of the MiG-17's fuselage could be pulled off, thus providing easy access to the engine, and its accessories. The Klimov-designed VK-1 was a single-spool turbojet with a centrifugal compressor. With the introduction of the afterburner on the MiG-17F, the engine's thrust increased by about 25 per cent (*VPAF Museum*)

A graduate of the Zhukovsky Aviation Institute, engineer Truong Khanh Chau was ordered to modify aircraft including the An-2, Mi-6 and MiG-17 during the war years (*Tran Dinh Kiem*)

unusual tasks. Rising to the rank of lieutnant-general, Chao always took an active interest in the development of the VPAF;

'I started work in the Nam Bo military factory as a locksmith back in 1952, only to find myself in the Technical College by 1955. By the end of the 1950s there was growing demand within the air force for better training, and to achieve this, some dual-stick conversion flying had to be carried out in the cockpit of the An-2 biplane. The task for this was given directly by Dang Tinh, from the Air Force Office, to the technical unit based at Gia Lam airfield, which I was part of. After successfully completing the modification, these An-2s served for many years as trainers.

'I enrolled in the Zhukovsky Aviation Institute in Moscow in 1960, after which I took part in a study tour in China. Once back in Vietnam, I was given more and more research subjects to undertake, and the air war required many modifications to our existing aircraft.

'For example, the air force high command wanted to send MiG-17s from secondary airfields against the American navy sailing off Dong Hoi. They intended to use bombs, but the MiG-17F had not originally been designed for this work. Therefore, we had to find a place for the bomb pylon, and then build in all the wiring for the release mechanism.

'Besides this, a brake chute housing was attached to the base of the rudder above the engine exhaust to achieve short landing runs. After three months of work the conversion was ready on two MiG-17Fs, which successfully completed their first mission on 19 April 1972. With the help of the brake 'chute, they were able to come to a full stop within 500 m.

'A few days after the attack the Americans located a secondary airfield, which was duly bombed. One aircraft was damaged, but the other "special" MiG-17 managed to get safely away to Gia Lam. In the wake of the raid, we received an order from the 923rd Fighter Regiment's commanding officer, Dao Dinh Luyen, to transport the damaged aircraft north. It proved impossible to work on the damaged jet during daylight hours due to constant American air raids, so one night the aircraft was disassembled, with some difficulty. Since we did not possess any cranes for loading the dismantled fighter-bomber onto awaiting trucks, we had to dig trenches for the vehicles to back into. Several tons of aircraft parts were then manhandled onto the flatbed trays of the four ZIL 6x6 trucks assigned to us. The MiG was then transported north to be repaired, test flown and returned to active duty.

'During the massive aerial campaigns of 1967-68, many of our aircraft were lost on the ground. In order to prevent this from happening again in 1972, the air force high command decided to disperse the MiGs to a variety of safe areas. The biggest challenge facing groundcrews was to find a means by which the jets could be moved both speedily and efficiently. One of the technicians suggested using the massive lifting capability of our Mi-6 helicopters, and after a lot of planning, and some testing, a special lifting device for the safe transportation of MiG fighters was built from steel rods, wire cables and leather belts. To guard against the rotation of an underslung MiG-17 whilst the Mi-6 was in flight, the jets were always transported with their speed brakes deployed – MiG-19s and MiG-21s had a special plate attached to avoud prevent this occurring.'

A valued servant of the VPAF during its struggle against the might of the American armed forces, Truong Khanh Chau achieved his Doctorate in 1973, and became director of the Vietnam Institute for Science and Technology upon its establishment in 1977.

The two NS-23 and single N-37D cannon of the MiG-17 were mounted in the same tray, together with their ammunition boxes and link ejection ports. The whole system could be lowered and lifted manually by turning a hand crank. This arrangement provided easy and quick access for loading and maintenance (*VPAF Museum*)

APPENDICES

APPENDIX A

AIR DIVISION AND REGIMENTAL NAMES OF THE VPAF

370th	**Hai Van**	Air Division	– **Pass of the Ocean Clouds** (North of Da Nang)
371st	**Thang Long**	Air Division	– **The Dragon Ascendant** (the name of Hanoi until 1831)
372nd	**Le Loi**	Air Division	– **Founder (1428-1524) of the Le Dynasty**
910th	**Julius Fucik**	Training Regiment	– **Czech Marxist publicist (1903-1943)**
917th	**Dong Thap**	Mixed Air Transport Regiment	– **Province in South Vietnam**
918th	**Hong Ha**	Air Transport Regiment	– **Old name of the Red River**
921st	**Sao Do**	Fighter Regiment	– **Red Star**
923rd	**Yen The**	Fighter Regiment	– **Hill of the Peaceful Site** (Ha Bac province, North Vietnam)
927th	**Lam Son**	Fighter Regiment	– **Blue Hill** (Le Loi's birthplace in Thanh Hoa province, North Vietnam)
935th	**Dong Nai**	Fighter Regiment	– **Province in South Vietnam**
937th	**Hau Giang**	Fighter-Bomber Regiment	– **Province in South Vietnam**

APPENDIX B

SIGNIFICANT DATES (INCLUDING ESTABLISHMENT OF UNITS) FOR THE VPAF

9 March 1949	**Air Force Research Committee** (Ban Nghien Cuu Khong Quan)
3 March 1955	**Airfield Research Committee** (Ban Nghien Cuu San Bay - C47)
End of 1956	**No 1 and No 2 Training Schools** (Truong Hang Khong So 1, 2)
24 January 1959	**Air Force Office** (Cuc Khong Quan)
1 May 1959	**919th Air Transport Regiment** (Trung Doan Khong Quan Van Tai 919)
30 September 1959	**910th Training Regiment** (Trung Doan Khong Quan 910) and
	Air Force Training School (Truong Khong Quan Viet Nam)
24 February 1960	**Parachute Company** (Dai Doi Khung Nhay Du - C45)
10 April 1961	**A-33 Aircraft Repair Facility** (Xuong Sua Chua May Bay A-33)
22 October 1963	**Air Defence Forces – Vietnamese People's Air Force** (Phong Khong - Khong Quan Nhan Dan Viet Nam)
3 February 1964	**921st Fighter Regiment** (Trung Doan Khong Quan Tiem Kich 921)
May 1965	**929th Bomber Squadron** (Dai Doi Khong Quan Nem Bom 929)
7 September 1965	**923rd Fighter Regiment** (Trung Doan Khong Quan Tiem Kich 923)
24 March 1967	**371st Air Division** (Su Doan Khong Quan 371) – 921st, 923rd, 919th regiments
October 1968	**929th Bomber Battalion** (Tieu Doan Khong Quan Nem Bom 929)
February 1969	**925th Fighter Regiment** (Trung Doan Khong Quan Tiem Kich 925)
3 February 1972	**927th Fighter Regiment** (Trung Doan Khong Quan Tiem Kich 927)
3 May 1973	**Mixed Air Group**
10 November 1973	**919th Air Transport Corps** (Lu Doan Khong Quan Van Tai 919) -1st, 2nd Air Battalion and 3rd Helicopter Battalion
30 May 1975	**935th Fighter Regiment** (Trung Doan Khong Quan Tiem Kich 935)
30 May 1975	**937th Fighter-Bomber Regiment** (Trung Doan Khong Quan Cuong Kich 937)
31 May 1975	**A-42 Helicopter Repair Facility** (Xuong Sua Chua May Bay A-42)
12 June 1975	**A-41 Transport Aircraft Repair Facility** (Xuong Sua Chua May Bay A-41)
5 July 1975	**918th Air Transport Regiment** (Trung Doan Khong Quan Van Tai 918)
20 July 1975	**917th Mixed Air Regiment**
15 September 1975	**372nd Air Division** (Su Doan Khong Quan 372) – 935th, 937th, 918th and 917th regiments
25 December 1975	**370th Air Division** (Su Doan Khong Quan 370)
31 May 1977	**Air Defence Forces** (Phong Khong Viet Nam), made independent of the VPAF
31 May 1977	**Vietnamese People's Air Force** (Khong Quan Nhan Dan Viet Nam), made independent of the ADF

APPENDIX C

NOSE NUMBERS OF VPAF MiG-15UTIs, MiG-17s AND MiG-19s

MiG-15UTI	JJ-5	MiG-17F and J-5	MiG-17F and J-5	MiG-17F and J-5	MiG-19S (J-6)
1920-????	*??-1505-??*	2001 to 2009	2110 to 2119	3001 to 3009	6010 to 6019
		2010 to 2019	*2130 to 2139?*	3010 to 3019	6020 to 6029
		2020 to 2029?	*2210 to 2219?*	3020 to 3029	6030 to 6039
	MiG-17 and J-5	2030 to 2039	*2230 to 2239?*		*6040 to 6049?*
	1030 to 1039	2040 to 2049	2310 to 2319		6050 to 6059
	1040 to 1049	2050 to 2059	*2330 to 2339?*	**MiG-17PF**	6060 to 6069
		2060 to 2069	2410 to 2419	4720 to 4729	
		2070 to 2079	2430 to 2439		
			2510 to 2519		
			2530 to 2539		
			2610 to 2619		
			2630 to 2639?		
			2710 to 2719?		

Numbers in italics are not confirmed

APPENDIX D

MiG-17 ACES OF THE VPAF

Name	Victories	VPAF aircraft	Regiment	Service
Nguyen Van Bay	Seven kills	MiG-17	923rd	1966-72
Luu Huy Chao	Six kills	MiG-17	923rd	1966-68
Le Hai	Six kills	MiG-17	923rd	1967-72
Nguyen Nhat Chieu	Six kills	MiG-17/21	921st	1965-67

APPENDIX E

MiG-17 AND MiG-19 PILOTS AND UNITS OFFICIALLY HONOURED AS HEROES

Tran Hanh	December 1966	921st 'Sao Do'	22 Dec 1969
Nguyen Van Bay	December 1966	921st, 1st Squadron	Dec 1966 and Aug 1970
Lam Van Lich	December 1966	921st, 3rd Squadron	18 Jun 1969 and 11 Jan 1973
Luu Huy Chao	December 1969	923rd 'Yen The'	3 Sept 1973
Phan Nhu Can	August 1970	923rd, 2nd Squadron	1 Aug 1970 and 31 Dec 1973
Le Hai	August 1970	923rd, 4th Squadron	Dec 1966, 18 Jun 1969 and 20 Dec 1979
Nguyen Nhat Chieu	December 1973		
Truong Khanh Chau	December 1973		

APPENDIX F

MiG-17 AND MiG-19 AERIAL VICTORIES

Date	Location	US Aircraft	US Aircrew	VPAF Aircraft	Regiment	Vietnamese Aircrew
03 Apr 65	Ham Rong	F-8E damaged	Thomas	MiG-17	921	Pham Ngoc Lan
03 Apr 65	Ham Rong	F-8		MiG-17	921	Phan Van Tuc
04 Apr 65	**Ham Rong**	**F-105D**	**Bennett**	**MiG-17**	**921**	**Tran Hanh**
04 Apr 65	**Ham Rong**	**F-105D**	**Magnusson**	**MiG-17**	**921**	**Le Minh Huan**
17 Jun 65	Nho Quan	F-4		MiG-17	921	Le Trong Long
17 Jun 65	Nho Quan	F-4		MiG-17	921	unknown
20 Jun 65	Mai Chau	A-1H		MiG-17	921	unknown
20 Jun 65	Mai Chau	A-1H		MiG-17	921	unknown
20 Jul 65	Tam Dao	F-4		MiG-17	921	unknown
20 Sep 65	Nha Nam	F-4		MiG-17	921	Nguyen Nhat Chieu

Date	Location	US Aircraft	US Aircrew	VPAF Aircraft	Regiment	Vietnamese Aircrew
14 Oct 65	*unknown*	*F-105D*	*Shuler*	*MiG-17*	*921*	*unknown*
06 Nov 65	**Hoa Binh**	**CH-3C**	**Lilly, Singleton Cormier, Naugle**	**MiG-17**	**921**	**Tran Hanh Ngo Doan Hung Pham Ngoc Lan Tran Van Phuong**
03 Feb 66	Cho Ben	A-1H		MiG-17	921	Lam Van Lich
03 Feb 66	Cho Ben	A-1H		MiG-17	921	Lam Van Lich
04 Mar 66	Yen Bai-Phu Tho	F-4		MiG-17	923	Ngo Duc Mai
26 Apr 66	Bac Son	F-4C		MiG-17	923	Ho Van Quy
26 Apr 66	Binh Gia	F-4C		MiG-17	923	Ho Van Quy
29 Apr 66	*unknown*	*A-1E*	*Boston*	*MiG-17*	*unknown*	*unknown*
05 Jun 66	unknown	F-8		MiG-17	923	unknown
05 Jun 66	unknown	F-8		MiG-17	923	unknown
21 Jun 66	**Kep**	**RF-8A**	**Eastman**	**MiG-17**	**923**	**Phan Thanh Trung Duong Truong Tan Nguyen Van Bay Phan Van Tuc**
21 Jun 66	**Kep**	**F-8E**	**Black**	**MiG-17**	**923**	**Phan Thanh Trung Duong Truong Tan Nguyen Van Bay Phan Van Tuc**
29 Jun 66	**Tam Dao**	**F-105D**	**Jones**	**MiG-17**	**923**	**Tran Huyen Vo Van Man Nguyen Van Bay Phan Van Tuc**
29 Jun 66	Tam Dao	F-105D		MiG-17	923	Tran Huyen Vo Van Man Nguyen Van Bay Phan Van Tuc
13 Jul 66	An Thi	unknown		MiG-17	923	Phan Than Trung
14 Jul 66	**An Thi**	**F-8E**	**Bellinger**	**MiG-17**	**923**	**Ngo Duc Mai**
19 Jul 66	unknown	F-4		MiG-17	923	Nguyen Ba Dich
19 Jul 66	**Vinh Phu**	**F-105D**	**Diamond**	**MiG-17**	**923**	**Vo Van Man**
19 Jul 66	Vinh Phu	F-105D	Steere	MiG-17	923	Nguyen Bien
29 Jul 66	**Hoa Binh**	**RC-47**	**Hoskinson+7**	**MiG-17**	**923**	**Luu Huy Chao**
05 Sep 66	**unknown**	**F-8E**	**Abbott**	**MiG-17**	**923**	**unknown**
05 Sep 66	unknown	F-8		MiG-17	923.	unknown
16 Sep 66	*unknown*	*F-4C*	*Robertson, Buchanan*	*MiG-17*	*unknown*	*unknown*
21 Sep 66	*unknown*	*F-4C*	*Kellems, Thomas*	*MiG-17*	*unknown*	*unknown*
02 Dec 66	Noi Bai	F-105D	Moorberg	MiG-17	921	unknown
05 Feb 67	Luong Son	F-4		MiG-17	921	unknown
26 Mar 67	Hoa Lac	F-4C	Crow, Fowle	MiG-17	921	unknown
19 Apr 67	**Suoi Rut**	**F-105F**	**Madison, Sterling**	**MiG-17**	**921**	**unknown**
19 Apr 67	Suoi Rut	F-105		MiG-17	921	unknown
19 Apr 67	**Suoi Rut**	**A-1E**	**Hamilton**	**MiG-17**	**923**	**Tan, Tho, Trung**
19 Apr 67	Suoi Rut	A-1H		MiG-17	923	Tan, Tho, Trung
24 Apr 67	Hanoi	F-4		MiG-17	923	Vo Van Man Nguyen Ba Dich Nguyen Van Bay Nguyen The Hon
24 Apr 67	Hanoi	F-4C	Knapp, Austin	MiG-17	923	Vo Van Man Nguyen Ba Dich Nguyen Van Bay Nguyen The Hon
24 Apr 67	Pha Lai/Son Dong	F-4B	Southwick, Laing	MiG-17	923	Mai Duc Toai Le Hai Luu Huy Chao Hoang Van Ky
25 Apr 67	Gia Lam	F-105D	Weskamp	MiG-17	923	Mai Duc Toai Le Hai Luu Huy Chao Hoang Van Ky

Date	Location	US Aircraft	US Aircrew	VPAF Aircraft	Regiment	Vietnamese Aircrew
25 Apr 67	**Hai Phong**	**A-4C**	**Stackhouse**	**MiG-17**	**923**	**Nguyen Van Bay** **Nguyen The Hon** **Ha Bon** **Nguyen Ba Dich**
25 Apr 67	Hai Phong	A-4E	Crebo	MiG-17	923	Nguyen Van Bay Nguyen The Hon Ha Bon Nguyen Ba Dich
25 Apr 67	Hai Phong	F-8		MiG-17	923	Nguyen Van Bay Nguyen The Hon Ha Bon Nguyen Ba Dich
12 May 67	**Hoa Lac**	**F-4C**	**Gaddis, Jefferson**	**MiG-17**	**923**	**Cao Thanh Tinh** **Le Hai** **Ngo Duc Mai** **Hoang Van Ky**
12 May 67	Hoa Lac	F-4C		MiG-17	923	Cao Thanh Tinh Le Hai Ngo Duc Mai Hoang Van Ky
12 May 67	Hoa Lac	F-4C		MiG-17	923	Cao Thanh Tinh Le Hai Ngo Duc Mai Hoang Van Ky
12 May 67	Vinh Yen	F-105D	Grenzebach	MiG-17	923	Duong Trung Tan Nguyen Van Tho
19 May 67	Xuan Mai	F-4B	Plumb, Anderson	MiG-17	923	Phan Thanh Tai
19 May 67	Xuan Mai	F-4B	Rich, Stark	MiG-17	923	Nguyen Huu Diet
20 May 67	*unknown*	*F-4C*	*Van Loan, Milligan*	*MiG-17*	*923*	*unknown*
23 Aug 67	Noi Bai	F-105		MiG-17	923	Cao Thanh Tinh
23 Aug 67	Noi Bai	F-105		MiG-17	923	Cao Thanh Tinh
23 Aug 67	**Noi Bai**	**F-4D**	**Carrigan, Lane**	**MiG-17**	**923**	**Nguyen Van Tho** **Nguyen Hong Diep**
25 Oct 67	Kep	F-105D	Horinek	MiG-17	923	Nguyen Huu Tao
19 Nov 67	**Hai Phong**	**F-4B**	**Clower, Estes**	**MiG-17**	**923**	**Le Hai**
19 Nov 67	**Hai Phong**	**F-4B**	**Teague, Stier**	**MiG-17**	**923**	**Nguyen Dinh Phuc**
19 Nov 67	Hai Phong	F-4B		MiG-17	923	Nguyen Phi Hung
14 Dec 67	Ninh Giang	F-8		MiG-17	unknown	unknown
17 Dec 67	**Ha Hoa**	**F-4D**	**Fleenor, Boyer**	**MiG-17**	**unknown**	**unknown**
17 Dec 67	Ha Hoa	F-4C	Brett, Smith	MiG-17	unknown	unknown
03 Jan 68	Thai Nguyen	F-4		MiG-17	923	Bui Van Suu
05 Jan 68	*unknown*	*F-105F*	*Hartney, Fantle*	*MiG-17*	*unknown*	*unknown*
14 Jun 68	Thanh Chuong	F-4		MiG-17	923	Le Hai
14 Jun 68	Thanh Chuong	F-4		MiG-17	923	Luu Huy Chao
19 Jul 68	*unknown*	*F-8*		*MiG-17*	*923*	*Le Hai*
09 Mar 71	unknown	Firebee		MiG-17	923	Luong Duc Truong
08 May 72	Yen Bai	F-4		MiG-19	925	Nguyen Ngoc Tiep
08 May 72	Yen Bai	F-4		MiG-19	925	Nguyen Hong Son
10 May 72	**Tuyen Quang**	**F-4E**	**Harris, Wilkinson**	**MiG-19**	**925**	**Pham Hung Son**
10 May 72	**Tuyen Quang**	**F-4D**	**Lodge, Locher**	**MiG-19**	**925**	**Nguyen Manh Tung**
18 May 72	Noi Bai	F-4		MiG-19	925	unknown
18 May 72	**Kep**	**F-4D**	**Ratzel, Bednarek**	**MiG-17**	**923**	**unknown**
23 May 72	Yen Bai	F-4		MiG-19	925	Pham Hung Son
23 May 72	Yen Bai	F-4		MiG-19	925	Nguyen Hung Son
11 Jul 72	**Pha Lai**	**F-4J**	**Randall, Masterson**	**MiG-17**	**923**	**Han Vinh Tuong**

Key

Vietnamese source

US source

Vietnamese source corresponding to US source

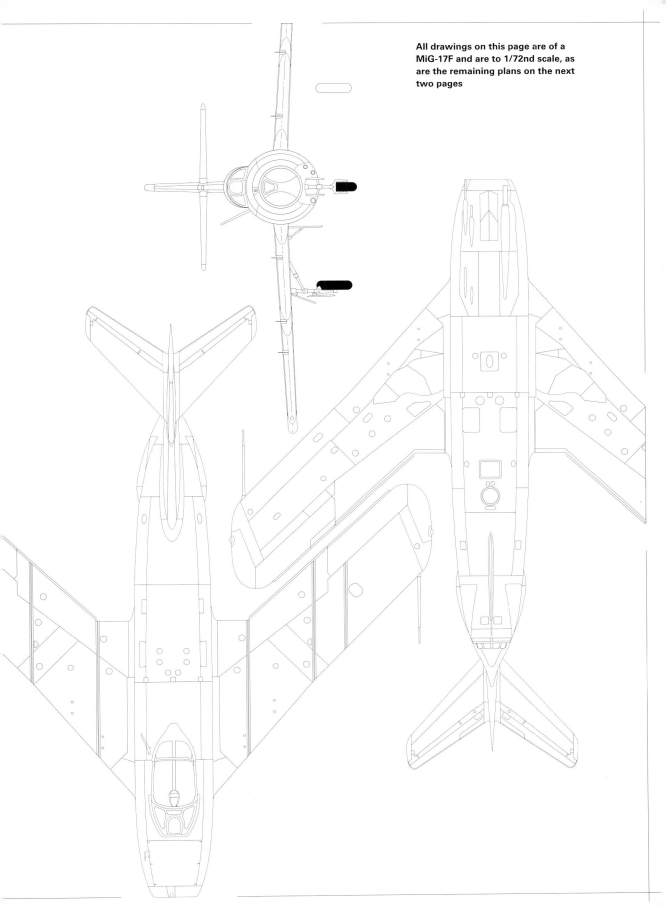

All drawings on this page are of a
MiG-17F and are to 1/72nd scale, as
are the remaining plans on the next
two pages

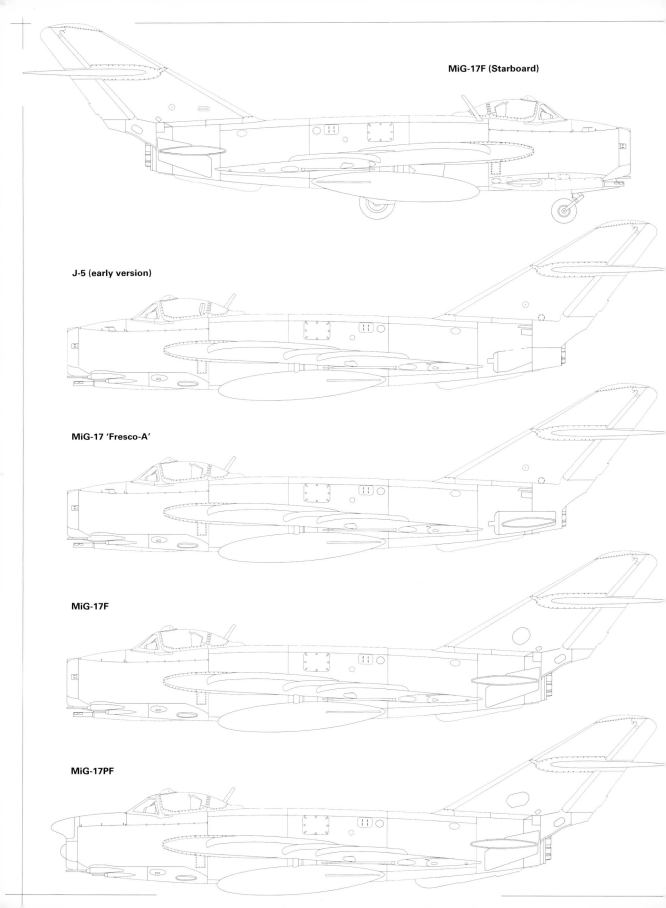

MiG-17F (Starboard)

J-5 (early version)

MiG-17 'Fresco-A'

MiG-17F

MiG-17PF

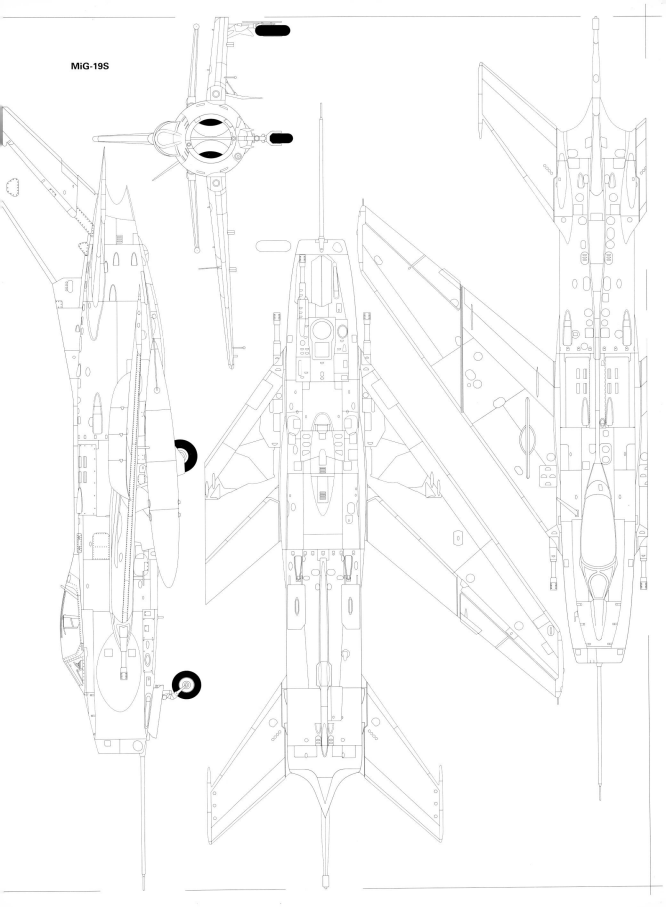

MiG-19S

COLOUR PLATES

1
Shenyang J-5 (MiG-17 'Fresco-A') 2614 of the 921st 'Sao Do', 1967
The first J-5s were exported to North Vietnam from 1964 onwards. This particular aircraft, which has been on display in the Nha Trang air base museum for many years, has prototype-style fuselage airbrakes.

2
Shenyang J-5 (MiG-17 'Fresco-A') 1036 of Le Minh Huan, 921st 'Sao Do', April 1965
Le Minh Huan used this J-5 to down Capt J A Magnusson's F-105D Thunderchief (59-1764, of the 355th TFW) over Ham Rong on 4 April 1965. He was in turn shot down just minutes later, either by another F-105 or an ADF SAM.

3
Shenyang J-5 (MiG-17 'Fresco-A') 1043 of the 921st 'Sao Do', 1966
The J-5 was a near-identical copy of the MiG-17, although it lacked an SRD-1M radar range finder and button ECM antennas. The airbrakes on the 'Fresco-A' were enlarged and repositioned lower on the fuselage in comparison with the later 'Fresco-C'. Its nose number beginning with '1', this Noi Bai-based J-5 was amongst the first batch of MiG-17s supplied to the VPAF in 1964.

4
Shenyang J-5 (MiG-17F 'Fresco-C') 2011 of Ngo Duc Mai, 923rd 'Yen The', 12 May 1967
This MiG-17 was used by Ngo Duc Mai to shoot down Col N C Gaddis and 1Lt J M Jefferson's F-4C Phantom II (63-7614, of the 390th TFS/366th TFW) over Hoa Lac on 12 May 1967. Marked with nine victory stars (denoting the number of kills scored by pilots flying '2011' perhaps?), the jet is currently displayed at the VPAF Museum in Hanoi.

5
MiG-17F 'Fresco-C' 2039 of Luu Huy Chao, 923rd 'Yen The', 24 April 1967
VF-114's Lt Cdr C E Southwick and Ens J W Laing were flying in F-4B Phantom BuNo 153000 (off the *Kitty Hawk*) over Pha Lai on 24 April 1967, when Kep-based Luu Huy Chao shot down their aircraft. Chao was credited with six aerial kills in MiG-17s whilst serving with the 923rd between 1966-68.

6 & 7
MiG-17F 'Fresco-C' 2019 of Le Xuan Di and MiG-17F 'Fresco-C' 2047 of Nguyen Van Bay, both from the 923rd 'Yen The', 19 April 1972
Fitted with a modified drag chute and pylons for two PROSAB 250-kg bombs, these MiG-17Fs were used as fighter-bombers in a special one-off mission over the Gulf of Tonkin on 19 April 1972. Flown by Le Xuan Di and Nguyen Van Bay, the jets took off from Gat and attacked the USS *Higbee*

and USS *Oklahoma City*. This was the first aerial attack on the US Seventh Fleet since World War 2. Bay's seven-victory marked 2047 is also currently on display in the VPAF's Hanoi museum.

8
Shenyang J-5 (MiG-17F 'Fresco-C') 2050 of Pham Ngoc Lan, 921st 'Sao Do', 6 November 1965
Assigned to the 'Red Star' regiment, and flying this aircraft, Pham Ngoc Lan joined Tran Hanh, Ngo Doan Hung and Tran Van Phuong when they downed a USAF CH-3C rescue helicopter on 6 November 1965. The helicopter was the 15th (and last) US aircraft credited to the VPAF in 1965.

9
MiG-17F 'Fresco-C' 2072 of the 921st 'Sao Do', 1968
MiG-17 fighters arrived in Vietnam either unpainted or in and overall light grey finish. To make them more difficult to spot both in the air and on the ground, a number of MiGs were subsequently sprayed in dark green camouflage, over which brown paint was liberally applied.

10
MiG-17F 'Fresco-C' 2077 of the 923rd 'Yen The', 1968
This 'snake-green' MiG-17F arrived (unpainted) at Kep in late 1965 as part of the second batch of 'Fresco-Cs' delivered to the VPAF. In the early days of the 'Yen The' regiment, there were no shelters at Kep, so virtually all of its MiG-17s were painted green and hidden under trees.

11
Shenyang J-5 (MiG-17F 'Fresco-C') 3003 of Tran Hanh, 921st 'Sao Do', 6 November 1965
Capt Tran Hanh flew this aircraft on the 6 November 1965 mission that saw a USAF CH-3C helicopter downed near Hoa Binh. Four pilots, including Hanh, were credited with its destruction.

12
MiG-17F 'Fresco-C' 3020 of Le Hai, 923rd 'Yen The', 14 June 1968
3020 displays no fewer than seven victory stars forward of the cockpit, this aircraft having been used by six-kill ace Le Hai when he claimed a Phantom II destroyed over Thanh Chuong on 14 June 1968. Hai stated that he hit the jet with two bursts of fire at an altitude of 2000 m, causing the F-4 to crash into the sea. US loss records fail to corroborate his claim, however.

13
MiG-17PF 'Fresco D' 4721 of Lam Van Lich, 921st 'Sao Do', 3 February 1966
With the installation of the RP-1 Izumrud locator in the MiG-17 in 1952, the 'PF' type gained all-weather and night-fighter capabilities. Lam Van

Lich proved the latter on 3 February 1966, when he claimed two A-1H Skyraiders shot down over Cho Ben – the first night victories for the VPAF. Again, these claims do not tally up with official US losses.

14
MiG-15UTI 'Midget' 1920 of the 910th 'Julius Fucik', 1965
The USSR presented 36 jets (MiG-17s and MiG-15UTIs) to the VPAF in 1963, with the handful of 'Midgets' serving exclusively with the 910th.

15
MiG-15UTI 'Midget' 2710 of the 910th 'Julius Fucik', 1964
As with all VPAF MiGs, this particular 'UTI' bore no unit or personal markings or emblems. The 'Midget' fleet remained unpainted throughout the jet trainer's long service in Vietnam.

16
Shenyang JJ-5 1505 of the 910th 'Julius Fucik', 1967
The Chinese-built JJ-5 trainer was an off-shoot of the J-5, and was not based on an original MiG design. It had a small radome mounted above the intake, which in turn meant that the S-13 gun camera had to be moved to the starboard side of the nose. The aircraft's armament was also restricted to a single 23 mm cannon on the underside of the starboard fuselage.

17
Shenyang J-6 (MiG-19S) 'Farmer-C' 6011 of Pham Hung Son, 925th Fighter Regiment, 10 May 1972
'Son B' used this J-6 to down F-4E Phantom II 67-0386 (of the 58th TFS/432nd TRW), crewed by Capts J L Harris and D E Wilkinson, over Tuyen Quang on 10 May 1972. Thirteen days later he claimed a second Phantom II over Yen Bai, which the communist regime stated was the 3600th enemy aircraft shot down over the North. This second kill has not been confirmed by US sources.

18
Shenyang J-6 (MiG-19S) 'Farmer C' No 6032 of Nguyen Hong Son, 925th Fighter Regiment, 8 May 1972
This was the 'Farmer' used by 'Son A' during the first dogfights involving the 925th, which occurred on 8 May 1972. He claimed an F-4 over Yen Bai that day (again unconfirmed by US records), but two days later his J-6 was downed by an AAM, and he died after ejecting over Tuyen Quang. No US crews claimed credit for 'Son A's' demise, so perhaps his jet was struck by an ADF SAM.

19
Shenyang J-6 (MiG-19S) 'Farmer-C' 6066, 925th Fighter Regiment, 1972
This natural metal J-6 was adorned with areas of dark green paint to prodcue a camouflage scheme similar to that seen on MiG-17s and MiG-21s. The first batch of 44 J-6s arrived in Vietnam in 1968-69.

COLOUR SECTION

1
This early production J-5 (MiG-17 'Fresco-A'), with prototype-style fuselage airbrakes, is on display in the Nha Trang air base museum (*all colour photographs by István Toperczer*)

2
The J-5 (MiG-17 'Fresco-A') displayed at the small museum in Hai

3
Ngo Duc Mai's J-5 (MiG-17F 'Fresco-C') has been a part of the VPAF Museum in Hanoi for many years

4
The MiG-17F 'Fresco-C' (formerly 2019) at Dong Hoi. This machine was one of two aircraft involved in the daring attack against the USS *Higbee* and USS *Oklahoma City* on 19 April 1972

5
The second of two MiG-17F 'Fresco-Cs' modified with a brake 'chute and loaded with two PROSAB 250-kg for an anti-shipping mission in 1972. It now resides in the VPAF Museum in Hanoi

6
This close-up view of Nguyen Van Bay's MiG-17F 'Fresco-C' at the VPAF Museum in Hanoi reveals seven faded victory stars beneath the cockpit

7
The Museum of the 4th Military District at Vinh includes this mouldering MiG-17F 'Fresco-C' (aircraft 2010) within its collection. The jet served with the 921st 'Sao Do' Fighter Regiment in the mid-1960s, and is fitted with the early-style ejection seat which lacked a face curtain

8
The VPAF Museum's J-6 (MiG-19S) 6058 was amongst the second batch of 'Farmer-Cs' supplied to the Yen Bai-based 925th Fighter Regiment by China in 1974

9
This numberless ex-925th Fighter Regiment J-6 is displayed at Da Nang air base. It is fitted with a K-13 Atoll AAM, this weapon having been supplied with the second batch of J-6s delivered to the VPAF from China in 1974. The Author is unsure if any of the original MiG-19Ss supplied to the VPAF in 1968-69 are still in existence

10
'Two Spot' (left side of the ZIL-157K truck) was the precision azimuth and elevation tracking radar, and 'Long Talk' (mounted on the right side of the truck) the air search and surveillance radar, of the Soviet-standard ground-controlled approach and aircraft recovery system, employed at most North Vietnamese air bases

INDEX

Figures in **bold** refer to illustrations
(commentary locators in brackets)